Premier Guides

Brecon Beacons
& The Heart of Wales

Above: View from Mynydd Illtud
Front cover: Black Mountain
Back cover: Elan Valley

Written by: Alf Alderson & Miles Cowsill

Revised and updated by: Alf Alderson

Photography: Wales Tourist Board, Chris Warren, Lily Publications

First published by Lily Publications 1995

Second (revised) edition 1996
Third (revised) edition 1997
Fourth edition 1998
This (revised) edition published 1999

Published by Lily Publications, PO Box 9, Narberth, Pembrokeshire, Wales SA68 0YT. Tel: (01834) 891461, Fax: (01834) 891463.
ISBN 1 899602 550.

Contents

Maps

Llanafan-Fawr

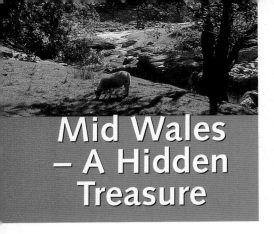

Mid Wales – A Hidden Treasure

Welcome to the fifth edition of this excellent visitor guide, which has been completely revised and updated and contains more information than ever.

The Premier Guide to Brecon Beacons & the Heart of Wales is unique - the only publication dedicated to these two neighbouring and spectacularly beautiful regions of the Mid Wales countryside.

As with all titles in the best-selling Premier Guide series, the emphasis throughout this new revised edition is on easy reading and quick reference. And to enable you to make the most of the guide, below are a few tips to help you get your bearings.

Brecon Beacons as used in the title refers to the area in and around the Brecon Beacons National Park; that is to say, from Abergavenny in the east to Llandeilo in the west, Hay-on-Wye in the north to Merthyr Tydfil in the south. This is a particularly wild and relatively untamed landscape, and we'd be the first to admit that words and pictures alone cannot even begin to convey the true spirit of this very special area.

The Heart of Wales is an appropriate and evocative term now used to promote the little-known countryside of Mid Wales. Here you will discover such delights as the Elan Valley and the rare red kite, the old market towns of Welshpool and Rhayader, and elegant Victorian spa towns such as Llandrindod Wells and Builth Wells. The region is even blessed with its own railway, the Heart of Wales line, which runs between Shrewsbury and Swansea and is a relaxing and enjoyable way to appreciate the true natural splendour of Mid Wales.

This handy guide gives you all the information you need to make the most of your visit to the Brecon Beacons National Park or the Heart of Wales. Attractions, places of interest, where to stay and where to eat, sports and leisure activities and facilities, maps, town plans, and a full A-Z of towns and villages: all of this and more can be found within these pages, providing essential holiday reading.

Look out too for the other renowned titles in the Premier Guide series, which include for 1999 the areas of Pembrokeshire, Carmarthenshire, Swansea & Gower, Cardiff and Cardiganshire.

Happy reading - and a very happy holiday!

Miles Cowsill, Managing Director
Lily Publications

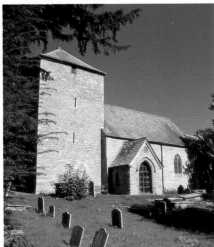

Llandefaelog Fach

CROESO

Mae hi yn wastad yn bleser cael croesawu ymwelwyr o rannau eraill o Gymru, a rydym yn hyderus y bydd y llawlyfr hwn o gymorth i chi i wneud y gorau o'ch gwyliau.

Mae'r gyfrol hon yn un o gyfres lwyddiannus *Premier Guides* a gyhoeddir gan wasg leol Lily Publications, a chaiff ei diweddaru'n gyson er mwyn cadw'r wybodaeth sydd ynddi mor gywir a chyfredol â phosib.

Hwn yw'r llawlyfr mwya cynhwysfawr y gallwch ei brynu ar gyfer y rhan hon o Gymru, gan ddod ynghyd, o fewn cloriau un llyfryn hawdd-ei-ddarllen, fanylion am lu o atyniadau naturiol ac o waith dyn. Mae'r rhain yn amrywio o harddwch cefn gwlad i gestyll o'r Oesoedd Canol, trefi a phentrefi o ddiddordeb hanesyddol arbennig, amgueddfeydd, gweithgareddau chwaraeon a hamdden, adloniant, bywyd gwyllt, gwyliau a digwyddiadau, a llawer llawer mwy.

Gallwch gadarnhau manylion agor, prisau mynediad ac ati yn uniongyrchol gyda'r atyniadau unigol (mae eu rhifau ffôn yn cael eu rhestru yn y llawlyfr) neu gyda'r Canolfannau Croeso lleol (sydd hefyd yn cael eu nodi).

Yn olaf, rydym yn sicr y gwnewch chi gytuno bod y canllaw hwn yn werth pob dimai. Felly mwynhewch ei ddarllen, a chofiwch gael gwyliau bythgofiadwy a fydd wrth eich bodd.

BIENVENUE

C'est toujours pour moi un immense plaisir d'accueillir des visiteurs dont la langue maternelle n'est pas l'anglais et nous espérons sincèrement que ce guide vous permettra de profiter au maximum de vos vacances. Faisant partie d'une série primée de *Premier Guides*, publiée par la maison d'édition locale Lily Publications, ce volume est mis à jour régulièrement dans le but de garder les informations qui y sont contenues aussi précises et actualisées que possible.

Il s'agit également du guide le plus complet de cette région du Pays de Galles vendu sur le marché, car il donne des renseignements pratiques sur une multitude de choses à faire et d'endroits à visiter, construits soit par la nature soit par la main de l'homme. Ces lieux de visite varient de la beauté du paysage de châteaux, de villes et de villages qui présentent un intérêt historique considérable, à des musées, des centres de sports et de loisirs, des lieux de divertissement, des parcs naturels, des festivals et autres spectacles et bien plus encore.

Des renseignements concernant les heures d'ouverture, les tarifs d'entrée et autres renseignements pratiques sont indiqués pour chaque lieu de visite (des numéros de téléphone sont donnés dans toute la brochure) ou dans les Centres d'Information Tourisme (qui sont également listés dans ce fascicule).

Nous sommes convaincus que vous trouverez ce guide indispensable et extrêmement complet pour son prix. Bonne lecture et passez des vacances inoubliables.

WELKOM

Het is altijd een eer om bezoekers welkom te heten die een andere taal dan het Engels spreken. We hopen van harte dat deze gids zal bijdragen aan een heerlijke vakantie.

Dit boek maakt deel uit van de serie *Premier Guides*, bestsellers uitgebracht door Lily Publications. Het wordt regelmatig herzien met als doel de opgenomen informatie zo accuraat en actueel mogelijk te houden.

Het is tevens de meest uitgebreide gids voor dit deel van Wales die er te koop is. Het brengt op eenvoudige wijze en in één band gegevens samen over een hele verzameling natuur- en door de mens gemaakte attracties. Deze variëren van de pracht van het landschap tot middeleeuwse kastelen, steden en dorpjes van groot geschiedkundig belang, musea, sport- en ontspanningsactiviteiten, amusement, natuur, festivals en evenementen, en nog veel meer.

Gegevens betreffende openingstijden, toegangsprijzen, enzovoorts kunnen rechtstreeks bij de individuele attracties (telefoonnummers in deze gids) of bij een plaatselijk Tourist Information Centre (Brits VVV-kantoor) (tevens in deze gids vermeld) worden nagegaan.

Tenslotte vertrouwen we erop dat u het met ons eens zal zijn dat deze gids zijn geld meer dan waard is. Dus veel plezier bij het lezen - en een plezierige en gedenkwaardige vakantie toegewenst.

WILLKOMMEN

Es ist uns immer eine große Freude, Besucher, deren Muttersprache nicht Englisch ist, willkommen zu heißen, und wir hoffen sehr, daß dieser Führer dazu beiträgt, das meiste aus Ihren Ferien zu machen.

Dieser Band aus der Reihe der bestverkauften Premier Guides des lokalen Unternehmens Lily Publications wird regelmäßig aktualisiert, um die darin enthaltenen Informationen so genau und so aktuell wie möglich zu halten.

Auch handelt es sich hierbei um wohl den umfassendsten Führer dieser Gegend von Wales, den Sie kaufen können und in welchem die Angaben zu der Unmenge an sowohl landschaftlichen als auch von Menschenhand geschaffenen Sehenswürdigkeiten in einem leicht zu lesendem Buch zusammengefaßt sind. Diese reichen von prächtigen Landschaften bis hin zu mittelalterlichen Schlössern, Städten und Dörfern von großem historischem Interesse, Museen, Sport und Freizeitaktivitäten, Unterhaltung, Tieren auf freier Wildbahn, Festivals und Veranstaltungen und manches noch vieles mehr.

Genaue Angaben zu Öffnungszeiten, Eintrittsgebühren u.s.w. können direkt mit den einzelnen Attraktionen (Telefonnummern sind im Führer angegeben) oder mit den örtlichen Fremdenverkehrsämtern (die Sie hier ebenfalls aufgelistet finden) verglichen werden.

Wir sind davon überzeugt, daß Sie mit uns einer Meinung sein werden, dieser Führer ist sein Geld wert. Wir wünschen Ihnen viel Spaß beim Lesen - und einen angenehmen und unvergeßlichen Aufenthalt.

The Brecon Beacons National Park

Centred on the highest ground in southern Britain, the Brecon Beacons National Park stretches 40 miles east to west from the Welsh border with Herefordshire, and 15-20 miles from the small country towns of Hay-on-Wye, Brecon and Llandovery, southwards over the mountains to the heads of valleys in South Wales.

The landscape consists of the Beacons themselves, a series of impressive peaks in the centre of the park rising to a maximum height of 886 m in Pen-y-Fan; wide expanses of moorland; deep cwms eroded by fast flowing mountain streams; broad valleys, ancient woodlands and sparkling rivers; and traditional architectural and historical features which make the area so unique.

The park's landscape has very much evolved through the interaction of people with nature over thousands of years - geology, wildlife, history, farming and other human activities have all played a part.

The designation of the area as a national park is official recognition that the Brecon Beacons and their surrounding are of the highest landscape quality, deserving both special protection and guaranteed opportunities to enjoy it, whether that involves a bit of effort such as hill walking or mountain biking, or nothing more than relaxing in the sun beside a gently flowing river.

The National Park Authority is responsible for ensuring that conservation and recreation are top priorities. Careful planning and sensitive management is needed to reconcile these two priorities with legitimate requirements of local communities to develop and move forward - this is a living landscape and not a museum! The Authority's staff includes an ecologist, archaeologist and building conservation officer as well as planners, a solicitor, a landscape architect, a graphic designer, wardens, administrators and information assistants. Volunteers bring extra skills and marvellous enthusiasm to many practical tasks.

The help of visitors is also essential in caring for the area, especially as the land is mostly privately owned and many local livelihoods depend on it. So please follow the Country Code wherever your exploration takes you.

Geology & Landscape

Four great blocks of Old Red Sandstone form the backbone of the park and the high peaks, producing the characteristic red colour of the rocks and soils. These rocks were produced by ancient rivers depositing sand in shallowing seas some 350 million years ago. Ripple marks can still be seen clearly in the rocks in some places. Great earth movements uplifted these deposits to form massive mountain chains. Since then, the forces of erosion have been constantly at work, wearing away all but the remnants we see today. The bands of rock visible on the steep northern faces of the Beacons show that the mountains are like the last fragments of a giant layered cake, most of which has already been devoured by time.

Pen y Fan and Corn Du are higher than the surrounding area, and marked by their distinctive flat tops. This is a 'cap' of harder, coarser sandstone and conglomerate (a mix of rocks deposited by fast-flowing rivers) that has protected the underlying 'weaker' rocks from the erosion suffered by the neighbouring landscape.

The snow capped Beacons

Not all of the park is sandstone, however. In the south there are bands of younger Carboniferous Limestone, Millstone Grit and Coal Measures rocks, aged between approximately 280 to 340 million years.

The broadest outcropping of limestone is around the village of Ystradfellte, along the courses of the rivers Mellte and Hepste. A whole series of spectacular waterfalls has been formed as these rivers cut down through the limestone to the harder Millstone Grit, resulting from the fact that limestone is soluble in water. Underground rivers are also sometimes found in the limestone areas, and these have formed caves and caverns as the water has eroded the rock over millennia.

You are never far from a textbook example of a geological feature. The impact of glaciers is seen in such features as huge cwms (valleys) gouged out by the action of ice; there are impressive scree slopes formed by the erosion over aeons of rock faces; gaping 'swallow holes' and dry river valleys occur in limestone country, formed by rivers that long ago sank beneath the earth - you don't have to be a geologist to appreciate the natural forces that shaped this unique landscape.

Wildlife

Although many parts of the national park look wild and untamed, the vast majority of the landscape is directly influenced by the activities of people. All the high land, for instance, is grazed by sheep, and sometimes by ponies. This year-round grazing, combined with harsh upland weather, greatly reduces the diversity of wildlife on the exposed mountainsides.

However, the cliffs and ledges which sheep cannot reach support a much richer flora, including some very rare arctic-alpine plants. These undisturbed ledges also provide nesting sites for ravens and the protected peregrine falcon. In some places, where it has been possible to reduce the grazing pressure, there are expanses of heather, bilberry and sheepís fescue. Birds of the

7

uplands include meadow pipits, ring ouzels, wheatears, curlews, snipe, lapwing and the occasional merlin, many of which you will see or hear when out on the hillsides and mountains.

The natural tree cover of the park is sessile oak and ash, and ancient woodland remnants support a huge range of plants and animals. The impressive red kite needs this kind of habitat for nesting, and as their numbers in Mid Wales increase they can now be seen in the central and western areas of the park as well as to the east.

Unfortunately, some slopes have been thickly planted with sitka spruce and other foreign conifer trees for timber production. Although such plantations provide homes for birds such as firecrests and crossbills, they do not support anything like the diversity of wildlife found in the native woodland that they often replaced.

Farmland on the lower slopes, with its distinctive patchwork of small fields and carefully laid hedgerows, is home to another, more adaptable group of plants and animals. One of the more unusual inhabitants here is the polecat. Buzzards are commonly seen over farmland, either soaring over the fields or watching from fence posts. Hedgerows rich with foxgloves, primroses, bluebells and stitchwort can be enjoyed along narrow lanes in late spring. The footprints of badgers and small mammals such as weasels may be spotted if you have a keen eye.

Llangorse Lake, the largest natural lake in South Wales, has lost some of the teeming wildlife for which it was known for hundreds of years, but it is still very important for its flora and fauna. Sometimes birds disturbed at Llangorse find refuge elsewhere: the shallow end of Talybont Reservoir is particularly good for wildfowl, and large numbers of wigeon, pochard, teal and various waders can be found there in winter.

The main river of the park is the Usk, which is famous for its salmon and trout, and begins its life in the wild moors of the western Brecon Beacons. From here it carves a spectacular valley as it flows west to east through the mountains. The Wye flows along the northern edge of the eastern boundary, and the Tywi forms the park's western border. Along these rivers and their many smaller tributaries are found dippers, kingfishers and grey wagtails, and at night elusive otters hunt along the banks.

The Past

The park is rich in sites that chart that area's history from the Stone Age to the present. Remains of chambered long cairns - the burial sites of Neolithic farmers - can be seen in the Wye and Usk valleys, the most accessible being beside the A40 on the north-west edge of Crickhowell. These date back to around 5,000 BC.

Bronze Age (3,000 BC) round cairns are found high on many mountains, including the tops of the Beacons themselves. Enigmatic standing stones and stone circles from these times are also found on moorland and lonely mountain passes, such as Maen Llia in Fforest Fawr. Wandering around these areas today it's not hard to imagine the hold they had on these early inhabitants of the area.

Later, Iron Age (1,000 BC) hillforts were built on defendable high ground, some probably functioning as permanent social, religious and market centres for the surrounding area. Garn Goch in the west of the park and Pen y Crug on the outskirts of Brecon are both good examples of the period. You'll find an excellent collection of inscribed prehistoric stones in Brecon's Brecknock Museum.

When the Romans invaded the area in the first century AD, they set up a series of military camps, the largest being Y Gaer, a few miles west of where Brecon was later built. Well-paved roads linked Y Gaer to other Roman camps, and the remains of such a track, know as Sarn Helen, can be seen on Mynydd Illtud Common.

The Norman conquest of Britain left its mark a thousand years later as Norman lords established their power-base by building a series of small castles and attempting to subdue the native population. Remains of Norman keeps can be seen at Bronllys, Crickhowell and Hay-on-Wye.

In the far west of the park, the enigmatic Carreg Cennen Castle changed hands many times, serving as both a Welsh and English stronghold in the turbulent 13th and 14th centuries.The circular keep at Tretower, near Crickhowell, is another reminder of this unsettled period of history. However, the associated manor house of Tretower Court, one of the finest surviving medieval houses in Wales, is the product of the more stable Middle Ages.

The park's heritage of religious buildings includes humble but endearing small churches such as Partrishow and Llanddeusant. These are often dedicated to Celtic saints of the post-Roman era. There are also remains of important priories at Llanthony and at Brecon, where the former priory church became the Cathedral of the Diocese of Swansea and Brecon in 1923. A heritage centre now interprets almost 1,000 years of its history.

Perhaps surprisingly, there are many reminders of the early industrial revolution within the park boundary. Water power from the rivers was harnessed at an early date to run machinery, and wood was used in charcoal furnaces; coke later provided steam power, and limestone served as a flux in iron founding. The most impressive remains are in the Clydach Gorge west of Abergavenny, and just south of the park boundary at Blaenavon.

The Monmouthshire and Brecon Canal is a reminder of the extensive system of horse-drawn tramways and waterways in South Wales which preceded the railways. They carried heavy raw materials and industrial products, and also brought lime into agricultural areas and took farm produce to markets in the expanding valley towns. If you want to know more about this hectic period in local history it's well worth visiting one of the museums in Brecon, Abergavenny or Merthyr Tydfil. They provide an interesting and comprehensive insight into the area's rural and industrial history during the industrial revolution.

Working in the Countryside

Farming has determined the look of the Brecon Beacons National Park for hundreds, maybe even thousands, of years. The patchwork of fields and hedges, the bare uplands, the valleys and woodlands have all been shaped by the pattern of farming life.

Most of the upland areas are common land. This often-misunderstood term does not mean that the land is owned by everyone. Common land belongs to a landowner in the usual way; what makes it different from an enclosed field or garden is that neighbouring farms have traditional rights in common to share use of the land. In practice this means that many local farmers have commoner's rights to graze sheep on the open mountains. This ancient farming system, which pre-dates the Norman conquest, only survived on the poorer quality high lands.

The most easily farmed valleys have been agricultural holdings for hundreds of years, and now provide improved grazing for sheep and some cattle. Hay, barley, silage and other winter feed crops are grown here. Methods of farming have changed rapidly across Britain in the past fifty years. Locally, the trend has been towards larger farms and silage rather than traditional hay meadows. Pastures have been ploughed up and re-seeded with rye-grass for improved sheep grazing, and traditional stone barns have often been replaced with much larger, prefabricated buildings.

As sheep subsidies are being reduced, many farmers are finding life difficult, and there is concern about the whole future of smaller family farms here. However, incentives are beginning to be introduced to encourage sound environmental management in farming, instead of just rewarding ever-increasing output.

Although sheep farming has dominated the park's landscape, other human activities have also left their mark. The high rainfall and steep-sided valleys made the area ideal for the creation of reservoirs. There are well over a dozen within the park, providing water for the heavily-populated towns of the South Wales valleys.

Many large catchment areas around the reservoirs, and other large areas of old woodlands or moorland were planted with conifers for timber production by the Forestry Commission and private forestry groups. A large number of the older blocks have recently reached productive maturity and have been felled in recent years. Forest Enterprise is taking this opportunity to 're-design' the forests more imaginatively, with more broadleaved trees in particular. This should benefit wildlife by providing a greater variety of habitats, as well as providing a more appealing and natural landscape.

The park also contains a few active limestone quarries and a silica mine, and on the southern boundary open cast coal mining is practised in a few places.

Recreation in the Countryside

In an increasingly busy and urban world, we all need a little peace and natural beauty. The Brecon Beacons National Park is perhaps best known for its fine walking country (see 'Walking in the Park'), although there are plenty of other ways of making the most of the great outdoors. Pony trekking is popular, and mountain bikers can also make use of the park's extensive network of bridleways and trails. Cyclists are also well catered for as the Welsh National Cycle Route (Lon Las Cymru) from Holyhead to Cardiff runs right through the area.

Watersports include canoeing on the canal, rivers and lakes, sailing and windsurfing on Llangorse Lake, and fishing for salmon, trout, perch or carp on rivers and reservoirs. Showcaves in the upper Tawe valley are well worth a visit, whilst more committed cavers will find plenty of challenges at sites such as Llangattock Mountain. There are some excellent nine- and eighteen-hole golf courses set amidst dramatic scenery - and for a more mellow time, Craig-y-nos Country Park has over 40 acres of woodlands, water and meadow to explore.

If you prefer your outdoor action to be a little more passive, there are plenty of excellent sites for bird watchers, botanists, archaeologists or artists to indulge their passion, whilst many of the ancient monuments and other countryside features described elsewhere in this guide are well worth a visit - from narrow gauge steam railways to forest centres and a rare breeds farms.

National Park and Tourist Information Centres can provide all the help and advice you may need, but for an introduction to the National Park and all it has to offer, you can't do much better than call in to the National Park Visitor Centre - the Mountain Centre - six miles south-west of Brecon. Admission is free, parking £1, the views are superb, family walks and events are organised through the summer, and the tea room serves very good food!

Further information on the Brecon Beacons National Park is available from:

Abergavenny National Park Information Centre, Monmouth Road, Abergavenny, Monmouthshire, tel. 01873

Brecon Beacons from Penderyn Road

853254 (seasonal).

Brecon National Park Information Centre, The Market Car Park, Brecon, Powys, tel. 01874 623156 (seasonal).

Llandovery National Park & Tourist Information Centre, King's Road, Llandovery, tel. 01550 720693 (open all year).

Craig-y-Nos Country Park, Pen-y-Cae, Swansea Valley, tel. 01639 730395 (summer only).

Village Information Agencies

You may also find the area's Village Information Agencies (VIA) useful. Their aim is to provide a wider network of information for visitors within the national park. They also help support village shops, and in choosing the agencies the National Park Authority has prioritised locations where the village shop is the only remaining facility within a community. You'll find the following information at the VIA locations: Internal information board about the national park with photos and information on the immediate area; publications and leaflets on the area; two reference packs of information - one on the national park, the other on local tourist information facilities. You'll find VIA's at the following locations:

Llangynidr Service Station & Post Office, Llangynidr, Crickhowell

The Post Office & Stores, Talybont-on-Usk

Rhos Filling Station & Shop, Pontneddfechan, Glynneath, Neath

Llythrdy (P.O.) Bethlehem, Bethlehem, Llandeilo, Carmarthenshire

Siop-y-Dyffryn, 15 Mountain Road, Brynamman, Ammanford

Govilon Post Office, Govilon, Abergavenny

Merthyr Post Office, Merthyr Road, Merthyr Tydfil

Cross Inn & Black Mountain Camping Site, Llandeusant, Llangadog, Carmarthenshire

The Village Shop, 5 Heol Tawe, Abercrave, Swansea

Spar Shop, Sennybridge, Nr. Brecon

Llanfihangel Crucorney Post Office, Llanfihangel Crucorney, Nr. Abergavenny

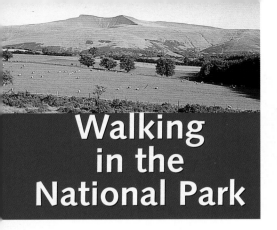

Walking in the National Park

There are few outdoor activities that you can't enjoy in the Brecon Beacons, but more than any other the area is known for it's walking. Whether you're setting out to tread along the high peaks and ridges or take a more leisurely jaunt along a quiet river valley, this is top class walking country.

The park covers an area of 519 square miles (1344 square km) and takes its name from the peaks at its centre. The highest is Pen y Fan, which rises to 2,907 feet (886m). A backbone of high ground forms four main mountain blocks - Black Mountains, Brecon Beacons, Fforest Fawr and Black Mountain (yes, the latter can easily be confused with the former!). This backbone runs right across the park westward from the English border, deeply cut by the broad, fertile valley of the River Usk between Brecon and Abergavenny.

It is made up of rocks of Old Red Sandstone for the most part, and along the park's southern edge narrow bands of Carboniferous Limestone and Millstone Grit have created dramatically contrasting scenery, characterised by cave systems of international importance and a succession of tumbling waterfalls. Little wonder that so many visitors are inspired to pull on those walking boots and head for the hills.

One of the safest ways to enjoy the wild beauty of the Brecon Beacons National Park is to join an organised walk, especially if you're new to the hills. These are led by National Park Authority staff and volunteers, with help from countryside organisations and landowners. There are many walks to choose from, especially in summer months, and the busy programme caters for all ages, abilities and interests.

Walks are classified to make the choosing easy (although the walking may not be!). For example, there are family walks, which are taken at a slow pace and are tailored to keep kids interested - or there's a choice of easy, moderate, energetic or strenuous walks, the latter including steep gradients requiring a good level of fitness.

You can get a copy of the season's walks programme from any National Park Information Centre, or by sending a stamped self-addressed envelope to the National Park Office, 7 Glamorgan Street, Brecon LD3 7DP. Booklets of walks are available from the Information Centres at modest cost.

Many walkers, particularly the more dedicated and experienced, prefer to go their own way. This is one of the finest ways to enjoy the hills, but you need to ensure on any walk - whether it's two hours or two days in length - that you're well prepared and equipped, that you treat the hills with respect and that you're aware of the possible dangers of being stranded in what can prove to be a bleak and lonely landscape.

Below are the basic guidelines for ensuring you enjoy a great day on the hills:

Plan your route

A map (of not less than 1:50,000 scale, approximately one and a quarter inch to the mile) is essential in planning a walk. The Ordnance Survey Outdoor Leisure series, with two double-sided sheets covering most of the national park, shows field boundaries and other important detail. Harveys also produce good walker's maps of the central and western areas of the park.

It's particularly important to keep to public footpaths and bridleways across enclosed farmland. These are shown on OS

Central Beacons

maps as broken lines - in red on 1:50,000 scale, in green on the 1:25,000 Leisure maps. Paths marked in black only are mostly private. Many public paths are signed at the roadside and waymarked along the route (yellow arrow for footpath, blue arrow for bridleway), but if in doubt ask permission first.

In some areas there is greater freedom to wander once open hill land is reached (National Park Information Centres can give you more precise details), but in most areas walkers have no legal right of access except on public paths.

When planning your route, allow for a speed of two and a half miles (4 km) an hour, plus at least an hour for every 1500 feet (450 m) climbed. Allow plenty of time to get to your destination before nightfall - and always have an escape route in mind in case of need.

Say where you're going

Make sure that all members of your group know the planned route and where you're aiming for. Leave details at your base of your intended route and approximate time of return. Telephone back to base if you're delayed or change your plans, and report promptly on return.

Check what you should take

Your list should include map, compass, watch, whistle, pencil and card (for notes), small first-aid kit, food and hot drink, reserve food (such as chocolate), waterproofs and extra woollens, and coins for the phone.

In the winter months (and on the hills Easter is often more like winter than summer!) everyone in the party should also carry a light bivouac bag, and a torch with spare bulb and battery. As a group you should also take a sleeping bag, stove and pans, and a group survival shelter.

Wear suitable clothes

The terrain on the hills is often rough and wet, so you need walking boots - or at the very least strong outdoor shoes/trainers with cleated soles. Warm and windproof clothing and reliable waterproofs should be taken even when the day looks good, as the weather can change with remarkable speed. Thin cotton jeans or shower-resistant clothing is useless in heavy rain and wind. In cold conditions woollen gloves and headgear are essential.

In winter you may also need an ice axe and crampons, but you need to know how to use them properly. If you don't you shouldn't be venturing onto the kind of terrain where they may be necessary!

Keep together

Never abandon anyone because they cant keep up! In fact you should let the slowest walker set the pace. It's a good idea (although not always possible) to ensure that there are at least four people in your group, so that if anyone is injured somebody can stay with the casualty and two others can go together for help.

Watch the weather

Never rely on the general forecast. It is local conditions which are important, and these can change rapidly on the hills. Mist, wind, rain or snow can destroy all sense of direction and cause serious dangers to anyone inadequately equipped. So always be sure of your bearings and, if caught in bad weather, keep close together and watch for signs of exposure or hypothermia in your companions. Such signs include fatigue, shivering, stumbling and slurred speech. If anyone is affected, follow the emergency procedure below.

In an emergency

Never try to move anyone who might be badly injured or is suffering from exposure. Keep the casualty warm and try to summon help by using the international distress signal - SIX blasts on a whistle, shouts, or flashes of a torch, repeated after a minute's pause (THREE are the reply). If you have to fetch help, leave someone with the casualty. To contact medical or rescue services, get to a phone and call 999 for the police, who will call out the necessary trained teams. When phoning be ready to give details such as the location of the casualty and time of the injury. Stay by the phone until rescuers arrive so that you can keep in touch with the co-ordinators, who might require further vital information from you.

This might all sound a little serious, but anyone who has been out in the hills when the weather takes a turn for the worse will know that there's often a thin line between having a rewarding experience - even in the worst of weather - and having a hideous experience.

So, kit yourself out properly and head for the hills - you'll have a great time!

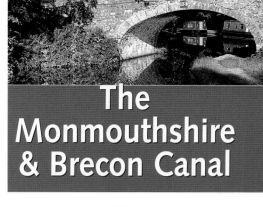

The Monmouthshire & Brecon Canal

One of the delights of the Brecon - Beacons National Park is the Monmouthshire and Brecon Canal, which runs from Brecon to Newport. The 'Mon and Brec', as it is commonly known, was originally two canals – the Monmouthshire Canal and the Brecknock & Abergavenny Canal – which joined end to end at Pontymoile, near Pontypool. The Monmouthshire section is itself not without interest but lies outside the area covered by this guide. By contrast, the Brecon and Abergavenny section lies almost wholly within the Brecon Beacons National Park, hugging the mountainside for much of the way as it follows the River Usk through beautiful scenery on its course towards Newport.

At Brecon, where a feeder from the Usk supplies the canal with water, a new theatre and terminal basins, funded by Powys County Council with a Strategic Development Grant from the Welsh Office, provide a much-improved start to the long truncated end of the canal. Leaving Brecon, the canal is at first on the north side of the river, with views across it to the Beacons. At Brynich the canal descends by a single lock before crossing the river on a massive four-arched aqueduct which is a scheduled ancient monument. A wooded section immediately above the river gives way to open countryside and final views of the Beacons before the canal moves toward the villages of Pencelli and Talybont. Drawbridges add interest along this section, culminating with an electric drawbridge across a busy minor road at Talybont. An embankment carries the canal through Talybont and past the wharf where the Brinore tramroad constructed by Sir Benjamin Hall (of Big Ben fame) brought coal and limestone to the canal.

The 375 yard (340 m) long tunnel at Ashford soon follows. To the left there are fine views across the Usk valley to Allt yr Esgair and Buckland Hill as the canal skirts Tor y Foel. At Llangynidr the canal drops down through a sequence of five locks, the top three in an attractive woodland setting. Meandering and river-side sections are followed by splendid views across Glan Usk to Myarth Hill and then Pen Cerrig-calch, with 'table mountain' set on its eastern flank. After Llangattock, where lime kilns are a reminder of the tramroad from the Llangattock escarpment, fine views of Pen Cerrig-calch slowly give way to Sugar Loaf.

Gilwern, in the parish of Llanelli, was once one of the busiest spots on the canal. The tramroad constructed by the B&A Company brought coal down to the canal from collieries in the Clydach valley and at one time sixteen boats a day carried coal towards Brecon and intermediate coal yards along the way. Other tramroads for the iron trade followed. Govilon wharf, now the headquarters of the Govilon Boat Club and the location of the British Waterways canal manager's office, also had tramroad connections as did Llanfoist. An evocative picture of the industrial scene at the latter, now so quiet and peaceful in its beautiful setting against the wooded hillside, is painted in Alexander Cordell's gripping novel Rape of the Fair Country.

After Llanfoist the canal rounds the head of the majestic Blorenge and there is soon a subtle change in the nature of the canal. Impressive views towards Abergavenny and the two Skirrids recede to give open views over the Usk plain. The villages of Llanellen,

Llanover and Penperlleni are bypassed, though only a short walk away, as the canal keeps on the higher ground necessary to join the Monmouthshire. The canal has a more isolated and lonely character, though none the less attractive for that. This is briefly enlivened by the boating activity at Goytre Wharf. Below Goytre the feeling of solitude is even greater until from Mamhilad onwards traces of industry and housing begin to draw near. Throughout the length of the canal, pubs offering food and real ale are never far away.

The canal has something to offer almost everyone, whether country lover, boater, walker, angler, or industrial historian. Handsome trees – oak, beech, sycamore, ash and sweet chestnut among them – share the banks with the ever-present alder. Springtime primroses, violets and celandines are followed by reed mace and yellow flag, rosebay, willowherb and foxgloves. Cherry blossom, rhododendron blooms, buddleia and rowan berries add their touch in season. Wild raspberries, elderberries, blackberries, hazel nuts and chestnuts are among the fruits available for the picking.

Every season of the year gives the canal a different face, and a winter's morning with the sun sparkling on frost-dressed trees is as attractive in its way as the colours of autumn or a golden summer's morn. The trees provide habitat for many common garden and woodland birds, among them tits, wrens, woodpeckers, nuthatches and treecreepers. Swallows swoop low over the water in summer; siskins feed on the alder cones in winter. Herons are a common sight at the water's edge and buzzards may often be seen over open countryside towards Brecon. For the lucky or the observant, the brilliant blue flash of the kingfisher is a treat.

Ducks – both mallards and 'bitzas' – grace the canal at many points; moorhens are often to be found where there are reed beds. Frogs and toads are common, and mink

Llanfoist

are all too often to be seen; correspondingly rare are the water voles. Pondskaters rush about on the surface of the water in summer and damsel-and dragonflies dart above it. For the angler with an Environment Agency rod licence, a variety of coarse fish – roach, dace, perch, bream, gudgeon, and mirror carp among them – await beneath the surface. Fishing rights along much of the canal are let to angling societies, but there are also unrestricted sections. Details of these, and the necessary fishing permit, can be obtained from the British Waterways office at Govilon Wharf.

For the experienced boater the navigable section, just over 34 miles in length (55 km), may seem short. Certainly it is possible to rush up and down the length of the canal in a few days at bank-damaging speed and see nothing. However, the discerning will find plenty to fill a week, while the 'energetically-challenged' will find that the small number of locks and the 23-mile-long lock-free pound from Llangynidr to Pontymoile – one consequence of the decision of the B&A

promoters to keep their canal at high level instead of descending by a series of locks to join the River Usk at Newbridge – will suit them too.

Boats for daily, weekly or part-weekly hire may be had from bases at several points along the canal – Goytre, Llanfoist, Gilwern, Llangynidr and Pencelli. Day boats may be hired at Goytre, Talybont and Pencelli, south of Brecon. For those wishing to enjoy the restfulness of the canal to the full, there are the alternatives of a cruise on a trip boat from Brecon, a horse-drawn boat from the canal museum at Llanfrynach, or a week on a pair of hotel boats.

For the visitor, the canal is accessible at many points, but car parking is not always easy. Convenient parking points include the British Waterways car parks at Govilon and Goytre. The latter's attractions include a craft and visitor centre, restored lime kilns and a picnic area. You can also hire boats and canoes here. Call 01873 881069/880661 for more details. The width and quality of the towpath vary, but improvements at several points, including Brecon, Talybont, Gilwern, Goytre to Llanfoist, Govilon and Pontymoile, have made the path more suitable for those in wheelchairs. Apart from the pleasure of following the towpath itself, other walks that use lengths of the towpath include the Usk Valley Trail, the Taff Trail and signposted local walks at Brecon, Llanfoist and Govilon. Cycling on the towpath is not generally permitted, but the section between Brecon and Brynich is open to cyclists.

Popular vantage points for motorists who want to view the canal with minimal walking are Brynich lock (parking available nearby in a layby with telephone box on the A40) and the locks at Llangynidr (limited parking on the bank by the bottom lock; alternatively in the Coach & Horses car park for patrons only). Boating activity at the locks is greatest early and mid-week and quietest on Fridays and Saturdays.

For the historian the canal, now a picture of peace and tranquillity, is a fine piece of 'liquid history'. The horse-drawn boats, approximately 63 ft long by 9 ft wide, crewed by a man and boy, and carrying up to 25 tons of cargo, have long gone and the once noisy wharves now see only pleasure boats. But for those with eyes to see and imagination to conjure with, there are buildings, tramroad remains and other relics of the past to evoke the scene as it was, when tens of thousands of tons of coal, lime and limestone, iron and other cargoes were carried on the canal each year. A visit to the Water Folk Museum near Llanfrynach will prove an entertaining and informative aid to visualising the past.

Both the Monmouthshire and the Brecknock & Abergavenny canals were largely the work of one engineer – Thomas Dadford junior, one of the family of canal engineers responsible for a number of canals in Wales and the English Midlands. The main line of the Monmouthshire was

completed in 1796; the Brecon & Abergavenny took rather longer. The Gilwern to Brecon section was completed early in 1801, but there was then a delay. The coal and lime trade towards Brecon was initially more important to the Brecon & Abergavenny Company than the iron trade towards Newport, and it was not until 1812 that the canal company minutes were at last able to record "The Committee set out to view the Canal towards Pontymoile and at Mr. Waddington's Boat House in Lanover, met him, and embarked there on board his Boat, and proceeded in the same all the way from thence to, and through, the Stop Lock at the Junction into the Monmouthshire Canal – being the first entrance from this Canal into that – amidst the acclamation of a very numerous body of the inhabitants as a token of their Joy at an Event so very beneficial to this County."

Viewed through the eyes of the many local shareholders, the two canals were a poor investment, partly because a toll-regulating clause in the B&A Act of Parliament for goods passing through to the Monmouthshire Canal encouraged ironmasters to lay tramroads to both canals, forcing the canal companies to compete and reduce tolls to barely economic levels. Trade was at its best in the 1820s and even then dividends on the B&A never exceeded 2.5%. Dividends slowly declined until railway competition all but killed trade in the 1850s. When the Monmouthshire (by now the Monmouthshire Railway & Canal Company) took over the B&A in 1865, shareholders received only £25 for their £150 shares. In 1880 the joint concern was taken over by the Great Western Railway.

In a wider sense the two canals were indeed a success. Together with their associated horse-drawn tramroads, they provided a transport network vital to the exploitation of the mineral resources of the region, linking quarries, mines, ironworks

Monmouthshire & Brecon Canal

and limekilns with manufacturing, agricultural, export and domestic markets. Prices fell and the availability of coal, lime, manufactured products and agricultural produce improved. Immense riches fell on wealthy landowners like the Duke of Beaufort, whose royalties on coal, iron ore and limestone extracted from his mountain land in the parishes of Llangattock and Llanelli (Gilwern) increased thirty fold in twenty years. Some of the wealth trickled down to those at the bottom end of the scale and the wealth and prosperity of the region as a whole rose.

Most of the Monmouthshire Canal is not at present navigable. Some of it lies culverted beneath Cwmbran; in other places bridges have been flattened. However, much tidying up and local restoration has taken place, parts are still 'in water' and most of the line can still be followed on foot. The Crumlin arm, which leaves the main line at Crindau, at the north of Newport, is well worth following to the Fourteen Locks Canal Centre and impressive flight of derelict locks,

weirs and side ponds at Rogerstone (Fourteen Locks is a scheduled ancient monument). Two lengths that have been restored to navigable condition are a short length at Gwastad, on the outskirts of Newport, and the most northerly two and a quarter miles approaching Pontymoile. Reconstruction of the culverted Crown Bridge at Sebastopol, essential to the latter length, and visitor moorings at Five Locks have been carried out by Torfaen County Borough Council, assisted by grants from the EEC, the Welsh Development Agency and Gwent County Council.

The entire Brecon & Abergavenny Canal, save for a short infilled initial length at Brecon, is navigable. It owes its survival largely to its continued use as a water feeder, long after through navigation had ceased in the 1930s, and to restoration by British Waterways in 1970. The cost of the restoration was jointly borne by the former Monmouthshire and Breconshire County Councils through the Brecon Beacons National Park Authority.

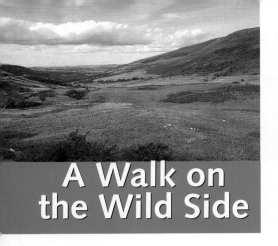

A Walk on the Wild Side

The Brecon Beacons landscape provides the ideal habitat for a wide range of birds, mammals and plant life. With uplands that bring to mind parts of Snowdonia, the Lake District and Exmoor, ancient woodlands, carpets of old hay meadows and a wild swathe of moorland reminiscent of Scotland's Flow Country it's not just humans who appreciate this landscape.

The area can be geographically divided into three main areas:

The north is dominated by the Cambrian Mountains, a wild upland plateau resounding with the 'too-ee' cries of golden plover and the bubbling songs of curlew. The bleak landscape is carpeted by purple moorgrass, heather and bilberry. Running off the hills, the waters have carved narrow and steep-sided valleys, often cloaked with slow-growing oak woodlands, above a blanket of mosses and lichens. These can best be seen in the Elan Valley Estate and the RSPB reserve on Corngafallt.

This is red kite country at its finest, a rich mosaic of woodlands, fields and hedgerows. Magnificent maiden oaks, some over 200 years old, provide suitable nesting sites, and the steep valley sides generate the up-draughts of air upon which the kites glide in search of their prey.

The 20th century was a hard time for the red kite: in the 1930s the population was reduced to a couple of breeding pairs. Numbers have increased since, but only slowly. Infertility brought about by inbreeding, the effects of pesticides and persecution, and changes in land management practices have all had an effect. In the face of such adversity it is wonderful that kites now number over 100 breeding pairs in Wales.

The middle section is similar in character to the north, but very different in use. Much of Mynydd Eppynt was cleared of its farming heritage 50 or so years ago to provide for a military training ground. In many respects the landscape has been fossilised as a result, revealing a countryside as it was moulded by early 20th-century farmers, farming by and largely without the aid of internal combustion engines. Many of the fields are small and surrounded by banks and walls. Some even show traces of ridge and furrow farming. The range is now shared by the military and sheep from neighbouring farms.

Access to the range is generally restricted to two roads. On any visit look for wheatears, which characteristically bob and bow on rocks and posts or dart from one to the other in search of insects. The most numerous bird is the meadow pipit, which unfortunately is the main prey item for the elusive merlin, which can sometimes be seen flying rapier-like low over the ground.

The third, most southerly and most spectacular of the three areas is that within the Brecon Beacons National Park. The park itself contains three distinct ranges: the (Carmarthen) Black Mountain or Mynydd Ddu, the Brecon Beacons central plateau (comprising Fforest Fawr and the Brecon Beacons themselves), and the Black Mountains. Rising to nearly 3000 ft (886 m), Pen-y-Fan is the highest of the peaks and is the dominant feature of the scenery.

The two very different rock types of the area (Old Red Sandstone to the north, Carboniferous Limestone and Millstone Grit

Brecon Beacons from Mynydd Illtud

to the south) make for an interesting juxtaposition of vegetation types, the former being alkaline in its influence and the latter acidic.

All three types of rock were formed during long periods when seas and brackish waters covered the land. They differ as a result of the variety of materials which settled out of the waters in which they were former, be they sand (Old Red Sandstone), the remains of corals and shellfish Carboniferous Limestone), or quartzites (Millstone Grit).

Purple moorgrass and matgrass are the dominant vegetation types, but cottongrass, heather and bilberry grow where the peat is deep. The lower slopes, however, are characterised by tall stands of bracken. The more exciting vegetation is often to be found in the more inaccessible places, such as crags and cliff faces. On the precipitous northern faces, Arctic-alpines such as purple

saxifrage, and plants like sea campion and roseroot, can be found. The plant communities are little changed from those which colonised the land immediately after the last Ice Age had shaped and scoured the rocks 10,000 years ago.

Buzzard and raven are the commonest of sights, but careful searching will reveal ring ouzel in the screes, or golden plover occasionally on the moors. Peregrine nest on the more inaccessible rock faces.

Flowing between and alongside these three upland massifs of the Brecon Beacons are the rivers and tributaries of the Usk and Wye. These rivers have carved deep channels, both narrow and broad, in the landscape. The valleys support lush vegetation, mainly grazing pasture for sheep, but where the sides are steeper rich broadleaved woodlands and large conifer plantations are found.

The rivers are teeming with wildlife.

Both the Usk and the Wye are famous for their salmon and trout fishing, thanks to waters that are relatively clean and have abundant insect life. Herons, kingfishers and dippers are also plentiful, although they are not so common in the upper reaches of river where acid rain can cause problems.

In some of the tributaries crayfish can be found, their population as yet unaffected by the more aggressive American species which have colonised some British rivers, and apparently free of the crayfish plague which has decimated numbers elsewhere.

On an evening walk near open water between April and October, you are likely to see bats flitting in and out of the trees and swooping low over the water as they catch insects. Stretches of the towpath of the Monmouth and Brecon Canal are a flurry of activity at dusk. A bat detector will pick up the noise of their echo location signals and reveal the identity of the species, which is not easy to do with the naked eye in the fading light. If you can catch a glimpse of a pale underbelly as it skims the surface of the water, this will be Daubenton's Bat.

The creature everybody wants to see is the otter. The Usk and the Wye are strongholds for this rare creature, but this was not always the case. Here as elsewhere the population of otters crashed alarmingly in the 1950's and 60's. The intensification of agricultural practices brought farming right up to the river banks and removed many of the bank side trees which provide cover and homes for otters. In addition, the rivers were polluted with pesticides which escaped from the land. The pollutants did not always kill the otters, but they caused reduced fertility and prevented successful breeding. The otter is a shy animal, easily disturbed, and its activity is now almost entirely restricted to the hours of darkness. But in the quieter stretches of river it may be possible to catch a glimpse of an otter at play during the daytime.

Mink are abundant, and not just along the main rivers. Seemingly bolder, these smaller cousins of the otter can often be seen vigorously searching the roots, nooks and crannies of the riverbanks. With care the two species can be readily distinguished. The mink is about half the size of an otter; at about 12" long it is more closely related to the weasel. An otter is nearer the size of a fox or small dog. In addition, the mink generally has black fur and the otter brown. It is possible to distinguish them in the water too. The mink is positively buoyant, floating like a cork with much of its body out of the water. The otter on the other hand swims with almost all of its body underwater. Once out of the water the mink appears bedraggled, its fur drenched. This is because it lacks the stiff 'guard hairs' which in the otter trap air close to the skin.

As well as the rivers and their tributaries, the area has over a dozen large water bodies, most of them man-made reservoirs storing drinking water for south-east Wales. There is, however, one natural and very special body of water - Llangorse Lake, or Llyn Syfaddan. Llangorse Lake is one of the most important lakes in Wales and was designated a Site of Special Scientific Interest in 1954 on account of its rich botanical heritage. Although over a mile long and half a mile wide, the average depth is only about 6-8 ft. The lake lies in a kettle-hole - a depression left in the land when permafrost and ice in the soil melted after the last Ice Age.

Llangorse Lake is unusual because of a combination of factors. The shallowness allows plants to grow throughout much of the lake. It is also eutrophic, which means that it is rich in nutrients and therefore highly productive for plant life. This in itself is unusual because the surrounding land or catchment is small in area, with little human population and low agricultural intensity. Chemically the lake is quite alkaline.

The vegetation is abundant and rich, and

Black Mountain

in places exhibits a pattern classically resembling that of successional processes. Ecological succession theory has it that shallow open bodies of water are colonised by floating-leaved plants. These are succeeded by emergent vegetation such as reeds and yellow flag iris. As the reedbeds dry out, they are invaded by alders and willows, forming a damp woodland or carr. Hence there exists a succession from open water to woodland. Behind the woodland, the unimproved fields are rich in varieties of marsh and spotted orchid.

The lake is also one of the most important sites in Wales for birds. It has the sixth largest reedbed, which in turn provides home for the second largest breeding colony of reed warbler (numbering up to 200 pairs). The reedbed provides refuge also for water rail, sedge and Cetti's warblers, and hundreds of roosting martins and starlings.

Great crested grebe, coot and mallard all breed on the lake, building their nests in the quieter areas away from boating and fishing activities. Careful management of the fields has led to the return of breeding lapwing.

During the spring and late summer all kinds of 'exotic' species may be seen. Ospreys are regular visitors, passing through on their way either to the breeding grounds of Scotland or their wintering quarters in Africa. Black terns and little gulls are also seen from time to time.

Of the reservoirs, Talybont is the most rewarding. It is near to Llangorse and probably provides safe refuge for many species when the recreational use of the lake gets too intense. Talybont reservoir is also a Site of Special Scientific Interest, and a local Nature Reserve. Its southern end is well worth a visit, for it is quite shallow and resembles Llangorse Lake in many ways.

23

Another man-made legacy providing a valuable habitat within the landscape is the conifer plantation. These are large tracts of forestry, several of which grow alongside the reservoirs. Although much maligned by many, these plantations provide the necessary conditions for a wide variety of species which would otherwise be absent from the area. Undoubtedly the increasing number of hobbies which return each year from Africa to feed on swallows, martins and dragonflies is a result of this mosaic of habitats. More residential though are the goshawks found in some of the secluded areas. They feed mainly on grey squirrels, but the odd pheasant or sparrowhawk does not escape them. Just occasionally come reports of crossbills, and another species more usually associated with the forests of Scotland, the pine marten.

The first grey squirrels reached the area in 1949; until then our native red squirrels were quite widespread. Today the last reds hang on in the large plantations of Mid Wales, finding there a refuge from their more aggressive American cousins.

In the newly harvested areas of plantations, two peculiar summer visitors can be heard more often than seen, especially at night. The grasshopper warbler and the nightjar both make strange churring calls which carry over long distances. The warbler is rarely seen, but the nightjar might be, quartering low over the ground at dusk and resembling a cuckoo in flight. During the day it sits tight on the forest floor, its plumage providing perfect camouflage.

The broadleaved woodlands vary according to location. Mostly they are oak woodlands rich with mosses and lichens, grasses or flowering plants. In the areas of limestone, ash is the major species, often with a dense understorey of hazel, and rare plants such as lily of the valley. Another speciality of the limestone is the whitebeam, of which there are three species found nowhere in the world other than perilously perched on the craggy cliffs of the area.. Alder woodlands grow in the damper areas and birch can be found higher up the slopes in the Brecon Beacons.

The woodlands are not as intensively managed as they once were. Even in the 1950's large areas would be coppiced - a method of cutting down trees which allows them to regenerate naturally with lots of stems. Often this provided fuel for local iron-ore smelters, or charcoal. The bark, especially of oak, was also valuable to give the tannins, essential material for treating leather.

In spring the woodlands are alive with the songs of warblers. Chiff-chaff, willow warbler and wood warbler can all be recognised with a little practice. Other species more often seen than heard include the pied and spotted flycatchers, and the redstart. The redstart's reddish-brown tail is unmistakable and is usually all that is seen as the bird disappears into the undergrowth.

Farming is the mainstay of the local community. Centuries of little-changed practices have yielded a patchwork quilt of small fields bounded by hedgerows and woodlands. This provides an ideal habitat for the sparrowhawk, the fox and the badger. Polecat, too, thrives in this kind of environment, but persecution, pollution and habitat change have reduced its population to the Welsh borders.

In a habitat such as this, with rabbits, sheep and plenty of small mammals, it's not surprising buzzards are present, and in large numbers. There may be well over 500 pairs of buzzard in the area, and on most days you'll see one wheeling, circling and gliding in the sky, calling with that familiar 'mew'. And in recent years the distinctive red kite with its noticeably larger wingspan and distinctive forked tail has also begun to reappear in the area.

Llanthony Priory

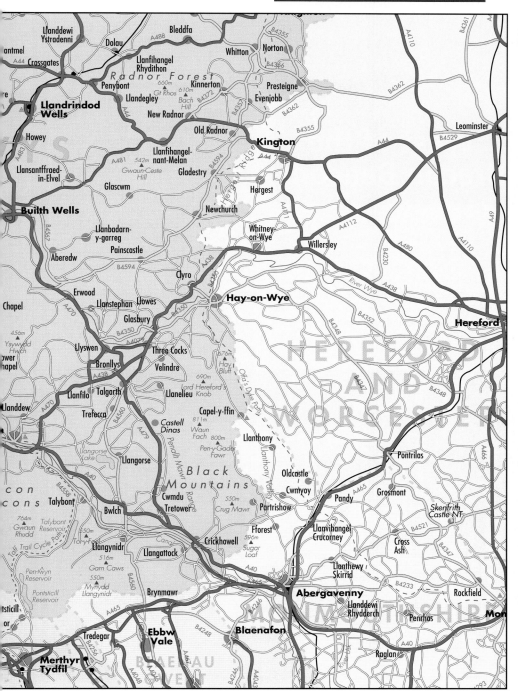

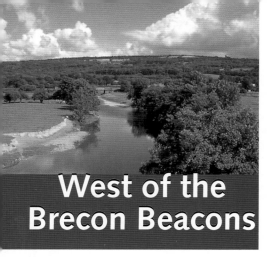

West of the Brecon Beacons

Immediately to the west of the National Park is the area formerly known as the borough of Dinefwr (pronounced Din-ev-oor). Now very much part of Carmarthenshire again under the local government reorganisation of 1996, the area is centred around the historic towns of Llandeilo and Llandovery and encompasses some of the most beautiful countryside in Wales.

In fact, this is definitely an area where you can find your own space: there are over six acres of countryside to every inhabitant – a fact readily apparent as you take in the sheer majesty of the scenery. The Cambrian Mountains rise to the north of the Vale of Tywi, while brooding to the south is the Black Mountain of the Brecon Beacons National Park. Birds of prey circle high above the landscape, among them the once-threatened red kite.

The Black Mountain, the Cambrians and the valleys of the Tywi and Cothi rivers are now the subject of signposted tours, designed to entice motorists off the beaten track. This is the way to discover the real Wales, taking you past such dramatic sights as the Llyn Brianne Reservoir – a man-made lake holding more than 13 billion gallons.

Dinefwr Castle was built in the 12th century and is sited on a rocky outcrop in the Vale of Towy, just a mile or so west of the market town of Llandeilo. It was the

Llandeilo

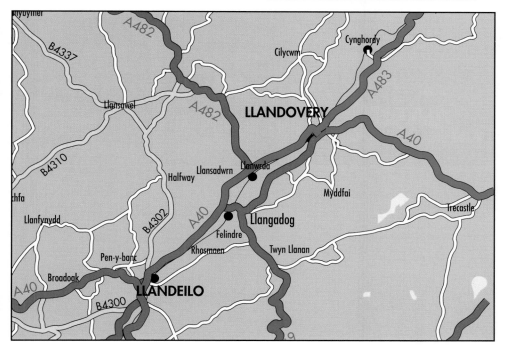

stronghold of Rhys ap Gruffydd, who successfully resisted the English invaders until Edward I brought the struggle to a violent conclusion at the end of the 13th century. During the reign of Henry VIII, the descendants of Rhys moved out of Dinefwr Castle and into Newton House, a stately home nearby. Rebuilt in the 17th century, this is now owned by the National Trust and is being restored; it is now open to the public. The castle itself is owned by Dyfed Wildlife Trust and is being repaired by Cadw to allow safe public access. Dinefwr Castle is not the only magnificent medieval stronghold still surviving in the area. One of the most dramatic is Carreg Cennen Castle, perched high on a rocky limestone crag 300 ft above the River Cennen. A few miles away is the hilltop ruin of Dryslwyn Castle, which stands within clear view of Paxton's Tower, a 19th-century folly. Llandovery also has its castle ruin, overlooking the town's car park.

Another attraction in the area is the Dolaucothi Roman gold mines at Pumpsaint, owned by the National Trust.

Llandeilo

The town of Llandeilo stands in rich farming land and is a fine centre for fishing and touring. The 19th-century stone bridge over the river measures 365 ft in length and has a central span of 145 ft. Originally of the 13th century, the church is dedicated to St. Teilo and was virtually rebuilt in 1840. Inside are two Celtic cross heads dating from the 10th or 11th century. The ruins of Dinefwr Castle lie one mile west, overlooking the Tywi valley. Golden Grove mansion – once the home of the Vaughan family – lies south-west and has been rebuilt. It now serves as the County Agricultural College. Another big attraction very close to Llandeilo is Gelli Aur Country Park, where you can enjoy a day exploring nature trails, a deer park and the famous arboretum.

This area is also noted for its

The Plough Inn

Renowned as a restaurant for 28 years Giulio and Diane Rocca welcome guests to dine in style and comfort. Local salmon, sewin, venison, Welsh lamb and beef are cooked simply or in delicious continental recipes. Whether it is a leisurely meal, a birthday or a family celebration our friendly staff will endeavor to make your visit a memorable one.

The Plough Inn is situated on the A40, a mile north of Llandeilo travelling towards Llandovery. Easily accessible either from the A483 and the M4 via Pont Abraham or the A476 from Cross Hands.

The Plough Inn, Rhosmaen, Llandeilo, Carmarthenshire SA19 6NP
Tel: 01558 823431   Fax: 01558 823969

concentration of traditional Welsh craft workshops and studios. For example, in Llandeilo a co-operative known as Crafts Alive stocks hundreds of hand-made creations, both practical and decorative, and up river in Llandovery the former Meat Hall has been transformed into a new craft centre. In addition, the Trapp Arts & Crafts Centre has a shop and display area within its workshops. Many local artists and craftspeople also extend a warm welcome to visitors who wish to see them at work in their premises.

The Trapp Art & Craft Centre, Llandeilo For more information ring 01269 850362.

Llandovery

The market town of Llandovery nestles at the top of the Tywi valley, surrounded by hills and unspoilt countryside. The main street has a small square with the Market House in the centre and a curious clock

Talley Abbey

tower standing next to it. Nearby, the Black Ox Inn recalls the days of the late 18th and early 19th centuries, when Llandovery was an important droving centre. Herds of black cattle were collected here and driven over the hills to the markets of England. The drovers were the first bankers of rural Wales; the Bank of the Black Ox issued its own notes. Llandovery is still very active in the cattle business, market days attracting farmers from all around. The town also has a Tourist Information Centre. Located within it is the impressive new heritage centre, which opened in 1996.

There are two notable churches in Llandovery, though both are located away from the centre. To the south is the parish church of Llandingat, which was restored in 1913, and about a mile north of the town centre is the church of Llanfair. Here a fine medieval tie-beam roof covers the nave, and the chancel has a barrel roof. The walls of the building are extremely thick, and the windows appear to have been placed quite haphazardly. There is modern glass in the east window and in the south side of the chancel. Both churches were restored by W.D. Caroe, who salvaged rather than rebuilt the structures.

Llandovery College, a big rugby rival of Christ Church in Brecon, is one of only two public schools in Wales. Built in the gothic style, it was founded in 1848 by Thomas Philips, who wished the Welsh language to be the basis of education.

Several roads converge on Llandovery and meet at the town. The road to the east, towards Brecon and the Usk valley, runs through a deep but narrow wooded gorge. The road to the south follows the fertile Tywi valley to Llanwrda and Llangadog, from which the route goes over the Black Mountain. The road due north follows the Tywi to its source in the wild country around Llyn Brianne. The north-east road takes the same course as the railway into central Wales. The railway crosses a high viaduct at Cynghordy and then tunnels under the pointed hill of the Sugar Loaf.

Another important town within the old borough of Dinefwr is Ammanford. Until the late 19th century, the Cross Inn at the centre of the town was almost the only building here. The town developed quickly because it is situated on the anthracite coalfield, and although the landscape is dotted with coaltips the surrounding area is not an industrial wasteland, as there is a great deal of agricultural land and some beautiful scenery, good views of which are afforded from a main road that runs over the Black Mountain to the Tywi valley.

Carmarthen

At the heart of the county is the ancient township of Carmarthen. It stands on the River Tywi, 8 miles inland – a position which

Carmarthen

inspired the Romans to make it their strategic regional capital. They also built an amphitheatre here, rediscovered in 1936 but first excavated in 1968. In legend, the town is the reputed birthplace of Merlin – wizard and counsellor to King Arthur.

Today, Carmarthen's quaint old narrow streets are full of Welsh character and tradition. There's also a first-class modern shopping centre with many familiar High Street names, complemented by Carmarthen's famous market. Open six days a week (main days Wednesday and Saturday), the market attracts people from all over Wales. The colourful atmosphere is enriched by the banter and barter of the adjacent livestock mart – Wales' biggest. You're also likely to catch more than a smattering of Welsh, as it is still widely spoken here. It is believed that the oldest manuscript in the Welsh language – The Black Book of Carmarthen, now in the National Library of Wales in Aberystwyth – was written in the town.

For sport, there's the town's modern leisure centre, with its outstanding all-weather facilities. A few miles west is a new venue for golfers, Derllys Court Golf Club, which has an interesting 9-hole par 35 course, set in a beautiful location amongst rolling countryside.

Another popular attraction which is virtually on Carmarthen's doorstep is the Gwili Railway, at Bronwydd Arms. This is one of only two standard-gauge steam railways in Wales, and a trip is pure nostalgia for adults and great fun for children. The train takes you to a wooded riverside area deep in the Gwili Valley. There is also a picnic site (refreshments are available at the station) and a delightful walk.

The Teifi Valley

Just fifteen miles north of Carmarthen is some of the finest walking country in all Wales – the wild open moorlands of the Llanllwni and Llanybydder mountains. This heatherclad paradise drops south to magnificently scenic Brechfa Forest, and west to the beautiful and spectacular Teifi Valley.

The Teifi Valley is rich in rural traditions and customs, with important market towns such as Llanybydder – famous for its monthly horse sales – and Newcastle Emlyn. There are also many attractions and beauty spots nestling alongside the river's winding course, notably Cilgerran, Cenarth Falls and Henllan Falls.

Just a few miles south-east of Cardigan and once a slate quarrymen's village, Cilgerran is now known for three things – the coracle, the castle and the new Welsh Wildlife Centre. Cilgerran Castle stands in a dramatic position on a high bluff above the River Teifi. Seen from the deep wooded gorge below – as it was for centuries by the coracle fishermen – it presents a spectacular sight which inspired great landscape artists such as Turner and Richard Wilson. Equally, the views which visitors can enjoy from its ruined towers are magnificent. The castle, small by comparison with Pembroke and the great Norman fortresses of North Wales, is mainly 13th century. Despite its apparently unassailable position, the castle changed hands many times between the 12th and 14th centuries. It was taken from the Normans by Lord Rhys in 1164; recaptured in 1204 by William Marshall; used as a base by Llewellyn the Great in 1215, when he summoned a Council of all Wales at Aberystwyth; taken again by the Normans in 1223, following which the present towers were built; and, after a period of decline and then refortification in the 14th century, was captured again for a brief period by the Welsh in 1405, during the uprising of Owain Glyndwr. The castle ruins are open to visitors and are well worth a visit. Cilgerran is also the venue for the annual coracle regatta, which takes place in August.

East of Cilgerran is the very pretty village of Cenarth, famous for its salmon-leap falls and one of the most popular beauty spots in the whole of West Wales. It is also recognised as the traditional home of the Teifi coracle, and here you will find the National Coracle Centre, which despite its name is a private enterprise, though no less important or interesting for that. Unspoilt Cenarth is a designated conservation area, with many of its buildings listed. The fine old bridge is believed to be 18th century, and the flour mill which houses the Coracle Centre dates from the 1600's. Also of historical interest is St. Llawddog's church and its mysterious Sarsen Stone. On the night of 23rd August 1944, this tranquil village had a rude awakening when a Wellington bomber of the RAF crashed on the river bank, killing four of its crew. Today, the only roar comes from the Teifi as it rushes over a series of falls into the deep salmon pool. Fishing is as popular here today as it has always been – though these days more from the river bank than the coracle – and other attractions in the village include the Salmon Leap - a small fishing museum and shop - and the Old Smithy Craftshop and Heritage Centre.

A little further east is Newcastle Emlyn a picturesque and bustling market town. It boasts a popular sports and leisure centre, and the Teifi is excellent for trout and salmon fishing. The castle of the name, now a ruin, dates back to 1240 and was built on the site of an old Welsh fortress. A few miles east along the river from Newcastle Emlyn is Henllan, another village known for its falls. But there is an even bigger attraction here – the narrow gauge Teifi Valley Railway. This uses both steam and diesel locomotives and offers a short but very enjoyable journey along the former GWR branch line that ran from Carmarthen to Aberystwyth. Just south of the Teifi Valley Railway, at Drefach Felindre, is the Museum of the Welsh Woollen Industry. At the beginning of the century the Teifi Valley was the very heart of the industry in Wales, with more than 40 mills working in the area. One of the most popular mills working today is Curlew Weavers, located near Rhydlewis, midway between Newcastle Emlyn and Llangrannog. This well-known, family-run mill produces a wide range of woollen fabrics and products, including tweeds, flannels, and curtain and upholstery materials. The shop, open all year round, has everything from bargain-price knitting wools to casual tops, skirts, dresses, coats, blankets and bedspreads. All are made from the finest hard-wearing wools, and Curlew Weavers will also work to your own designs.

Carmarthen Bay

South of Carmarthen, the River Tywi emerges into Carmarthen Bay alongside the rivers Taf and Gwendraeth. This is an area of outstanding natural beauty, where scores of waders and seabirds take rich pickings from the broad expanse of mudflats formed by the three estuaries. It also marks the beginning of a glorious 50-mile stretch of Carmarthenshire coastline that in the west embraces Pendine Sands, once famous for the world landspeed record exploits of Sir Malcolm Campbell and others, and in the east boasts the magnificent award-winning beach of Cefn Sidan Sands. Beyond this the coast extends to the environmentally-important mudflats of the Loughor estuary and the town of Llanelli .

It is here that you will find one of Wales' most famous towns - Laugharne, a charming medieval township where the great poet and writer Dylan Thomas spent the latter years of his tragically short life. His home was the Boat House – his "seashaken house on a breakneck of rocks", standing above the estuary – which is now a Heritage Centre dedicated to his memory. Born in Swansea in 1914, he died in New York on 9th November,

1953. But Laugharne was the place he most loved and which inspired much of his best work, including Under Milk Wood. Laugharne Castle, dating from the 12th century, was largely reconstructed in the Tudor period and became a mansion in 1782. In 1939, when the tenant was novelist Richard Hughes (author of A High Wind in Jamaica), Dylan Thomas stayed in the castle's gazebo ("the romantic, dirty summerhouse overlooking the marshes") and wrote Portrait of the Artist as a Young Dog. The castle, now restored and open to visitors, was once the retreat of pirates. It was also captured single-handedly – albeit on canvas – by the great British landscape artist J.M.W. Turner. Laugharne's Town Hall, with its distinctive white tower (and "the clock that tells the time backwards") is where the Town Corporation – founded by medieval charter in Edward I's reign – still meets in ancient tradition, presided over by the Portreeve.

From Laugharne, the road west cuts a picturesque route to Pendine Sands. The attractions here, apart from the superb beach, include the new Museum of Speed - a permanent reminder of the resort's contribution to motorsport history.

Waterfall Country

At its northern end, the beautiful Vale of Neath extends into the foothills of the Brecon Beacons National Park. This is known as waterfall country – famous for the number and variety of its spectacular falls, which are unique in Britain and much admired for more than two centuries by a succession of artists, poets, writers, photographers and now film makers too.

The best-known and most accessible falls are those at Melincourt and Aberdulais, as well as the seventeen enchanting cascades created at Gnoll Country Park, Neath, by Herbert Mackworth in 1740.

Many more waterfalls are to be found in the wooded valleys and deep gorges of the rivers Mellte, Hepste and Nedd, between the villages of Pontneddfechan and Ystradfellte, on the southern edge of the Brecon Beacons. The only way to see them is on foot, and the car park of the Angel Inn in Pontneddfechan is the ideal starting point.

The easiest of the walks from here is to the falls at Sgwd Gwladys. Some of the other eight falls in the area can be more difficult to get to, particularly in wet and slippery conditions, and the National Park Authority points out that visitors should be aware of the potential hazards presented by such a spectacular landscape. The Authority, which has produced a useful leaflet entitled Waterfall Walks in the Ystradfellte Area, also recommends that you should not attempt to explore the falls unless properly dressed and equipped for walking. Another informative publication is the full-colour booklet Waterfall Walks in the Vale of Neath, while the new edition of Ordnance Survey Outdoor Leisure Map Number 12 is an invaluable guide to serious walkers in the area.

The nine falls in the Pontneddfechan area are Sgwd Gwladys and Sgwd Einion Gam on the River Pyrddin; Horseshoe Falls, Lower Ddwli Falls and Upper Ddwli Falls on the Neddfechan River; the Sgwd-yr-Eira Falls on the River Hepste; and the falls of Lower, Middle and Upper Clungwyn on the River Mellte.

Aberdulais Falls

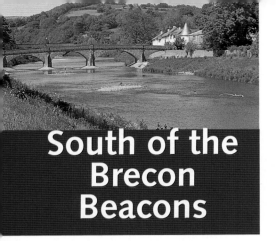

South of the Brecon Beacons

Aberdare

This industrial town of Mid Glamorgan lies at the head of the Cynon Valley, west of Merthyr Tydfil. Ironworks and coal mines gave the town prosperity in the mid-19th century, but since 1972 the nearby glaciated valley which became the site of nineteen mines has been transformed into the Dare Valley Country Park. Covering an area of 500 acres, this had the distinction of being the first country park in Wales. The hillsides, moorlands, woods and lakes support a great diversity of wildlife, and waymarked trails radiating from the visitor centre and residential complex provide perfect opportunities to savour the park's unspoiled countryside and to take in the superb views.

Tower Colliery This colliery is situated in Hirwaun, a village close to Aberdare. The Tower Colliery has a history that goes back over 200 years, as the only serving coal mine that worked through the era of Iron Masters and steam coal era when Wales led the world, until the modern anthracite era of smokeless fuels.

By 1994 the colliery was the last deep open mine in South Wales and after a determined battle by the miners the pit was closed on 22nd April 1994. Most people thought it was the end for the mine but the miners thought differently, and went on in the next eight months to form a company called T.E.B.O (Tower Employee But Only).

They raised £2,000,000 of their own money in a bid to save the pit. Against all odds they won the bid to own the pit, against eight other bidders. Since then Tower has proved itself to be a winner, the colliery has not only created 340 jobs but has moved on to become a vibrant new coal company.

Today it has its own visitor centre where the visitor can take a cup of tea or a meal with miners in their canteen.

Abergavenny

Though just outside the park boundary, the busy market town of Abergavenny is the gateway to the Brecon Beacons National Park – and indeed to Wales. To the north is Sugar Loaf (1,950 ft) and to the north-east is Ysgyryd Fawr, on which stand the remains of a chapel dedicated to St Michael. To the south-west, Blorenge (1,832 ft) is a good viewpoint. The beautiful River Usk flows just to the south of the town and runs roughly parallel to the Monmouthshire and Brecon Canal. The Romans had a fort here and the foundations of this are thought to lie under the castle mound.

The castle was founded by Hameline de Balun late in the 11th century. It was captured in 1215 by Llywelyn the Great, extensively damaged during the Glyndwr uprising, and destroyed by parliamentary forces in 1645. The few remains date from the 13th and 14th centuries and consist of two broken towers, the gateway, and fragments of wall. The interesting town museum is situated in the castle grounds.

Abergavenny's main street contains buildings from many periods. Especially noteworthy are the 19th-century Angel hotel, which was an important coaching inn, and the gothic-revival town hall. Other interesting buildings in the town include the 16th to 17th-century King's Arms Inn; the early 19th-century King's Head Inn and

Westbury is building new homes in

great locations

throughout South Wales.

ABBOTS WALK, MARGAM.
2, 3 & 4 bedroom homes.
TELEPHONE (0973) 745355

ALLT IOAN - JOHNS WOOD, CARMARTHEN.
2, 3 & 4 bedroom homes.
TELEPHONE (01267) 232591

BEAUFORT PARC, LLANELLI.
3 & 4 bedroom homes.
TELEPHONE (01554) 834580 / 835300

BENEDICT COURT, ABERGAVENNY.
2 bedroom luxury apartments.
TELEPHONE (01873) 858563/853534

BUCKLAND DRIVE, BWLCH.
3 & 4 bedroom homes.
TELEPHONE (01874) 731053

CANDLESTON GRANGE, BRIDGEND.
4 & 5 bedroom executive homes.
TELEPHONE (01656) 663905

CLÔS REBECCA, LLANNON, NR. LLANELLI.
4 & 5 bedroom executive homes.
TELEPHONE (01269) 831056

COED DUON RISE, BLACKWOOD.
2, 3 & 4 bedroom homes.
TELEPHONE (01495) 230283

CWRT CEFN YDFA, MAESTEG.
3 & 4 bedroom homes.
TELEPHONE (01656) 732342

FORGE MILL, YSTRAD MYNACH.
2, 3 & 4 bedroom homes.
TELEPHONE (01443) 862205

HUNTERS RIDGE, TONNA.
2, 3 & 4 bedroom homes.
TELEPHONE 0831 543138

MANOR PARK, BEDWAS.
2, 3 & 4 bedroom homes.
TELEPHONE (01222) 889608

MARINERS COURT, CARDIFF.
1 & 2 bedroom apartments.
TELEPHONE (01222) 342312

OAKBROOK MEADOWS
DÔL NANT DDERWEN, BRIDGEND.
2, 3 & 4 bedroom homes.
TELEPHONE (01656) 766493

SILVERDALE, SWANSEA.
2 & 3 bedroom homes.
TELEPHONE (01792) 798083 / 702507

ST JAMES PARK, ABERDARE.
3 & 4 bedroom homes.
TELEPHONE (01685) 876959 / 874356

ST MARYS PARK, ROGIET.
4 & 5 bedroom executive homes.
TELEPHONE (01291) 431235

THE PADDOCKS, DRAETHEN.
3 & 4 bedroom homes.
TELEPHONE (01633) 440653 / 440316

THE TUDORS, PENPEDAIRHEOL.
2, 3 & 4 bedroom homes.
TELEPHONE (01443) 835045 / 835010

TIRCOED FOREST VILLAGE, PENLLERGAER.
2, 3 & 4 bedroom homes.
TELEPHONE (01792) 894902 / 899943

TRAHERNE VILLAGE, PENYLAN.
4 & 5 bedroom executive homes.
TELEPHONE (01222) 483064

TY DRAW CWRT, PONTPRENNAU.
2, 3 & 4 bedroom homes.
TELEPHONE (01222) 731066

ALL SALES OFFICES OPEN 7 DAYS A WEEK
11AM-5PM NOV - FEB, 11AM-6PM MARCH - OCT
New for 1999: **CHEPSTOW, RAGLAN, ROGERSTONE,**
BARRY, CARDIFF WATERFRONT, NEATH & ABERAVON.
TELEPHONE (01222) 761414 for details.

adjoining medieval arch; and the Old Court, a house dating from 1500 built into the old town walls. St Mary's Church in Monk Street is the town's most important piece of architecture. Originally it was the church of a Benedictine priory founded in the 11th century, but today only the tythe barn and prior's house remain of the priory buildings. The church contains many treasures, including 24 choir stalls dating from the late 14th century and a huge wooden figure of the patriarch Jesse in the Lewes chapel. Several fine tombs dating from the 13th to 17th centuries can also be seen in the building.

The road (A465) four miles north of the town passes the ancient hamlet of Llanfihangel Crucorney, under the slopes of the Skirrid. Here the Skirrid Inn, the oldest in Wales, has retained its medieval construction. Nearby is the Tudor mansion of Llanfihangel Court, with a beautifully

Abergavenny

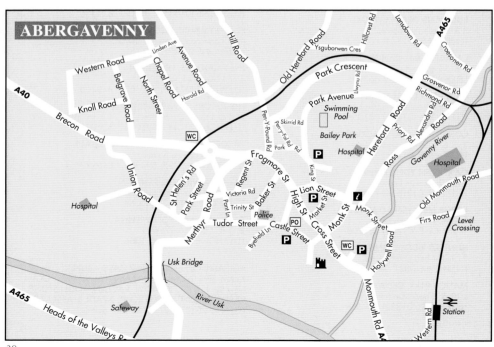

Nr Trecastle

furnished interior. Charles I was entertained here during his unhappy visit to Wales in the final stages of the first Civil War. It is open occasionally during the summer months.

Abergavenny Museum The Castle, Castle Street. Tel: 01873 854282.

Abergavenny Castle Castle Street. Tel: 01873 854282.

Hill Court Gallery Entry is free during exhibitions open every day except Mondays.

Blaenafon

Coal mining and iron dominated this town in the past; today they still play a role, as the local coalmine and ironworks are open to visitors. The Big Pit, which closed in 1980, is now open to visitors as a museum. The workings of the former coalmine are intact and accessible, and there is also a mining gallery which illustrates methods of coal extraction, as well as an underground guided tour at the mine conducted by ex-miners. Blaenafon Ironworks, opened in 1789, is also open to visitors. The blast furnaces and workers' cottages can be viewed at this historically-important site.

Big Pit Mining Museum Telephone 01495 790311.

Blaenafon Ironworks Telephone 01495 792615.

Caerleon

The town of Caerleon lies four miles up the Usk from Newport and is one of the most historic in Wales, boasting strong associations with the Romans and King Arthur. The town was one of the three foremost legionary bases in Britain, the others being Chester and York. The fort covered five and a half acres, and the outline of the ramparts can be clearly traced on the west and south-west sides, although houses still cover the rest of the site. The parish church stands on the foundations of the old basilica, and a large section of the wall and the legionary barracks can be seen in the Prysg field. The showpiece, however, is the Roman amphitheatre, excavated by Sir Mortimer Wheeler in 1920. In the Middle Ages, it was covered with grass and known as King Arthur's Round Table. That powerful romancer, Geoffrey of Monmouth, cast Caerleon in the role of King Arthur's Camelot and Tennyson, the poet, came here to capture the Arthurian atmosphere when he was writing the 'Idylls of the King'. More recent excavations have exposed the remains of the Roman Baths, which are interpreted in a new exhibition centre at the site.

Caerleon Legionary Museum
Tel: 01633 423134.

Caerleon Roman Amphitheatre
Tel: 01633 421656.

Caerleon Roman Fortress Baths
Tel: 01633 422518.

Greenmeadow Community Farm, Cwmbran This community farm, unique in Wales, was established in the 1980's to help protect one of the last green spaces of Cwmbran from the spread of urban development. The original fully-refurbished 17th-century farmstead has 150 acres of land throughout Cwmbran and offers an invigorating rural retreat in an urban setting. A day at the farm is great fun for everyone, as there is always something new to see. Attractions include traditional farm animals, rare breeds, pets corner, an exhibition barn with a barn owl and young chicks, woodland trails which offer sightings of fallow deer and a great variety of wildlife, demonstrations of crafts and country skills, and amenities such as tea rooms, restaurant, teaching facilities,

and rooms for meetings, conferences and parties. For more information ring 01633 862202.

Grosmont
An old-world village set on a hillside, Grosmont stands amid beautiful scenery by the River Monnow on the border between Gwent, Hereford and Worcester. The single street of the village runs between the castle and the church. Grosmont is small by today's standards and is an important centre for anglers. The church of St Nicholas carries a massive octagonal tower topped by a spire, and has a large unfinished nave arcade. Inside there is a huge flat-faced stone knight which is thought to be an effigy of one of Edmund Grouchback's descendants.

Grosmont Castle was one of three castles erected in the vicinity by the Norman Lords of Abergavenny to protect the Welsh/English border; the others are Skenfrith and White. It is believed that the castle at Grosmont dates back to 1163. The structure was largely

40

rebuilt during the reign of Henry III, who stayed here for a time until Llywelyn the Great stormed the building and forced Henry and his queen to escape at night. In 1410 Owain Glyndwr burned the town and seized the castle, establishing Rhys Gethin here to hold the position. English reinforcements were hurriedly sent under the command of Harry Monmouth (later to be Henry V),and the Welsh were completely routed. The castle is now under the care of Cadw (Welsh Historic Monuments), and little remains of it except the inner ward gateway, the keep, the containing wall with two drum towers, and a 13th-century octagonal chimney which once served the banqueting hall.

Merthyr Tydfil

Merthyr Tydfil takes its name from St Tydfil, daughter of the Lord of Brycheiniog (Brecon) who is believed to have been martyred for her Christian faith by pagans in AD 480. The town is situated in the Taff valley. It became an iron and coal town and records show local iron workings here as early as the 16th century. By 1831 Merthyr Tydfil had become the largest town in Wales. In 1804 the first steam locomotive made its journey between Merthyr Tydfil and Abercynon, built by the Cornish engineer Richard Trevithick. Penydarren Works produced the first rails to be made in Wales, for the Liverpool and Manchester Railway, and later made cables for the Menai Bridge.

After the First World War heavy industry moved out of the town to areas near the coastal seaports, and Merthyr Tydfil was left in a desperate situation with half the population unemployed. The community is now supported by light industries. Cyfarthfa Castle was built in 1825 and now serves the town as a museum and art gallery. The parish church of St. Tydfil, of 14th-century origin, has undergone a great deal of alteration. It

contains three inscribed stones, one of which dates from around the 9th century. The composer, Dr Joseph Parry was born in Merthyr Tydfil in 1814, and Keir Hardie, the pioneer of socialism, was the town's MP during the early years of the 20th century. To the north of the town is the Brecon Beacons National Park and the Garw Nant Forest Centre.

Joseph Parry's Cottage 4 Chapel Row.Tel: 01685 723112.

Ynysfach Engine House Tel: 01685 723112.

Brecon Mountain Railway A magical narrow gauge railway located at Pant. Tel: 01685 722988.

Cyfarthfa Castle Museum Tel: 01685 723112.

Garwnant Forest Visitor Centre Situated off the A470, 5 miles north-west of Merthyr Tydfil.

Llancaiach Fawr Living History Museum This award-winning family attraction enables you to follow in the footsteps of Charles I, who visited here on 5th August 1645. Stewards from the gentry household of Colonel Edward Pritchard, dressed in authentic period costume, guide you round this splendid semi-fortified manor, embellishing the experience with intriguing tales of life in a civil war stronghold. Visitors are invited to dress in period clothing too, and to try on the armour. You can even take a turn in the stocks! Llancaiach Fawr is also the setting for a programme of special events throughout the year, including ghost tours, murder mystery evenings and a 5th August anniversary celebration to mark Charles I's visit during those turbulent Civil War years. For more information ring 01443 412248.

41

FACTORY OUTLET SHOPPING

UP TO

50% OFF

HIGH STREET PRICES

Festival Park Factory Outlet Shopping Centre has over 30 shops selling top brands in fashion, footwear, giftware and toys at fantastically low prices. With restaurants and superb parkland it's a great day out for the whole family.

Opening Hours: Monday-Saturday 10.00am-6.00pm. Open Sunday 11.00am-5.00pm.

On the site of the Garden Festival of Wales, Ebbw Vale, Gwent, South Wales. Tel: 01495 350010. Follow the brown & white Festival Park signs.

FACTORY OUTLET SHOPPING

Festival Park, Ebbw Vale This beautiful landscaped park, of more than 63 acres, boasting hillside woodlands and wetlands, lakes and formal gardens, is unique to the area. It still has many Garden Festival features of 1992, but also includes beautiful country walks, public works of art, gardens and special environmental centres to make an enjoyable and interesting visit for young and old alike.

Festival Park has its own Visitor Centre (and café) where you can discover more about the 'Iron Barons', the industrial boom of the 19th century, the thrills and excitement of Garden Festival Wales, and the subsequent plans for the future of the new Victoria village development.

The gardens include many interesting features. For example, tucked up in the hillside overlooking the park is an exceptional opportunity to explore the hidden depths of pondlife at the wetlands. In addition, in the woodlands, visitors can experience how man can live in harmony with the environment. Enjoy the Tree House, a man-sized bird's nest, a snake maze and a willow dome.

Not everything at Festival Park is orientated towards the British way of life. The park includes an Oriental Pavilion which has been built to demonstrate the characteristics of Far Eastern architecture. A tropical planthouse contains many exotic and carnivorous plants from Malaysia and Singapore, as well as cacti, succulents and Mediterranean plants.

There is plenty for the family to explore at the exciting Festival Park, which is open all year round, seven days a week, between dawn and dusk. Admission is free. For further information, and up-to-date details of a full Events Programme, telephone 01495 350010.

Where in Wales was...

The first ballot box used?

The first steam engine to run on rails?

The Mabinogion translated into English?

Laura Ashley born?

The first Labour MP elected?

'Myfanwy' composed?

The Red Flag first flown?

Find out at Cyfarthfa Castle Museum & Gallery
Merthyr Tydfil – full of surprises!

Telephone 01685 379 884 for a FREE information pack or complete and return the coupon:

Name _____

Address _____

_____

_____ Postcode _____

Post to:
The Tourism Section, Merthyr Tydfil County Borough Council, Castle Street, Merthyr Tydfil CF47 8AN

Talybont Reservoir

Parc Cwm Darran Country Park This peaceful country park, just three miles south of Merthyr Tydfil, has many attractions: caravan and camping site, an excellent choice of outdoor activities, visitor centre and coffee shop, education centre and children's environmental Watch Club, exciting annual programme of events, wide variety of wildlife, and facilities for disabled visitors. For more information ring 01443 875557.

Parc Bryn Bach, Tredegar This once-desolate area of land that was scarred by a long period of opencast coal mining has been transformed in the last fifteen years to become one of Wales' most popular country parks, annually attracting over a quarter of a million visitors. The 36-acre lake and surrounding woodland and grassland forms the core of the park, along with a purpose-built Visitor Centre. Other attractions here include a children's adventure playground, a 30-pitch touring caravan and camping site,

and an 18-bed self-catering bunkhouse. For those visitors who wish to make the most of the park's great outdoor, there are several activities on offer, from angling and orienteering to boardsailing, waterskiing and hang-gliding. For more information ring 01495 711816.

Monmouth

Monmouth is a market town and has many Tudor and Georgian buildings in a network of old streets. Three rivers flow round the town – Trothy, Monnow and Wye – giving it a stategically important position from which the whole of South Wales could be controlled. Hence the Romans had a base near Monmouth, and the town was a vital link in the network of Roman roads that ran one way through Caerwent and Caerleon and another way to Wrexham, Caersws, and Chester. Long after the Romans, the Normans made the town a springboard for

their penetration of South Wales, and the first lords of Monmouth were Bretons.

Monnow Bridge, situated in the town centre, is the only Norman fortified bridge to survive in Britain. The fortified tower is on the bridge itself and was built in 1260 as one of the four medieval gates into the town. The bridge has three semi-circular arches with a total span of 38 yards and each arch has three wide ribs. The bridge was originally constructed for pedestrians and horses only. More than anywhere else in the borderlands area known as the Welsh Marches, Monmouthshire has remained mostly Welsh in the use of language and place-names. In fact, Wales has now recovered one of its lost provinces, as the county is once more known by its title of Gwent.

The original castle here was probably a simple wooden structure on a motte, but no definite trace of either remains. Monmouth was listed in the Domesday Book of 1086 as part of Herefordshire, and was the headquarters of the Marcher Lordship of

Monmouth

Monmouth. Henry Somerset, son of the second Marquis of Worcester, built Great Castle House on the site of the old castle's Round Tower in 1673. By 1801 the house had become a girls' school, and in 1875 it started its career as the headquarters of the Royal Monmouthshire Engineer Militia. Restoration of the castle's medieval remains which peacefully rise above the River Monnow was begun by the government in 1913, and both castle and house are open to visitors. The former castle was the birthplace of Henry V.

Shire Hall is situated in Agincourt Square and was built in 1724 on the site of an Elizabethan Market Hall. Until 1939 the assizes were held here, and in 1839 John Frost and the Chartist leaders were tried here for high treason after the Newport riots. A statue of Henry V was placed in a recess of the wall of the Shire Hall in 1792. Alongside this statue is one of Charles S. Rolls, founder of Rolls Royce and a pioneer airman, who was the first person to fly the English Channel both ways without landing.

Monmouth's Nelson Museum contains a comprehensive collection of material associated with Lord Nelson – including sextants, Nelson's fighting sword, and models of his ships. To the east of the town a wooded hill known as Kymin (840 feet) is surmounted by an 18th-century Round House and Naval Temple. The temple was visited by Nelson in 1802 and commemorates a galaxy of admirals unequalled by any other age or country. Excellent views over the Monnow and Wye valleys are afforded by Kymin. The site is run by the National Trust.

The parish church of St Mary retains a decorated-style tower and spire, but the rest of the church was the work of G.E. Street in 1881, who replaced a Georgian church built by Francis Smith of Warwick. The church of St Thomas has a fine Norman chancel arch, an original north door, and a 19th-century

Raglan Castle

pseudo-Norman porch. The interesting font and galleries were made from timber supplied by the Duke of Beaufort. The part of the town where St Thomas's Church is sited is known as Overmonnow, and was once a centre for cap-making. The close-fitting caps from here were the 'Monmouth Caps' mentioned in Shakespeare's Henry V. The River Monnow has coarse fish and trout and attracts many keen anglers. Monmouth Agricultural Show is held annually at the end of August.

St. Peter's Church at Dixton, near Monmouth, is on a site that was an ancient place of worship. This church has been subject to severe flooding, and brass plates on the north side of the chancel arch record heights of three high floods.

Gwent Wildlife Trust, Monmouth
Gwent Wildlife Trust was established in 1963 to purchase and protect its first nature reserve, Magor Marsh – the last remnant of fenland on the Gwent Levels. Since then the

Trust has acquired over thirty of the most treasured wildlife sites in the region. Management of these reserves forms only part of the work, as the Trust also offers help and advice to industry, local authorities, landowners, schools and individuals, to encourage the conservation of plants and animals both common and rare. Gwent Wildlife Trust is a registered charity and a member of the RSNC Wildlife Trusts Partnership – the largest voluntary organisation concerned with all aspects of wildlife protection. For more information telephone 01600 715501.

Monmouth Castle For details contact the local Tourist Information Centre.

Monmouth Museum Tel: 01600 713519.

Pontypool
This industrial town was the centre of a predominantly coalmining and tinplate

district, and in 1720 became the first town in Britain to successfully produce tinplate. About two miles east is Llandegfedd Reservoir, which supplies water to Cardiff and is used for sailing and fishing. The Monmouthshire and Brecon Canal runs for over thirty-three miles from Pontypool to Brecon.

The Valley Inheritance Tel: 01495 752036.

Raglan

Raglan Castle was erected on the site of an 11th or 12-century motte and bailey structure. The present building dates from 1430 to the early 17th century and the Great Yellow Tower of Gwent is one of its oldest parts. The parish church has a pinnacled tower and contains a few mutilated effigies of the Somersets, damaged during the siege of the castle by Cromwell's troops. The castle is open to visitors and is run by Cadw. One of the two interesting windows displays various coats of arms. Three miles west is the fine Regency mansion of Clytha House, and about four miles west-north-west is the notable early 18th-century Pant-y-Gotre bridge over the River Usk.

Raglan Castle For more information ring 01291 690228.

Vale of Usk & Wye Valley

The Vale of Usk is the pastoral heartland of Gwent. It is centred on the river, which cuts a winding course from the high, rugged landscape of the Brecon Beacons through meadows and farmland to Newport. Whether you explore the vale by car or on foot, the views are spectacular and the attractions are many, taking in the market towns of Abergavenny and Usk. One of the most rewarding ways to appreciate the vale's charms is to enjoy the Usk Valley Walk, which follows the course of the river between Caerleon and Abergavenny.

To the west of Newport is Chepstow - the first town in Wales - where the River Wye runs out into the Severn estuary. The Wye Valley, acclaimed by many as the most romantic valley in Wales, is an Area of Outstanding Natural Beauty. Among the many visitors drawn to the region since the late 18th century was William Wordsworth, whose love of the valley inspired him to write Lines Composed a Few Miles Above Tintern Abbey in 1798. The valley is beautiful at any time of year, and you can explore it on foot, by car or even by canoe.

The Vale of Usk and Wye Valley merit a visit for their magnificent scenery and wealth of historic treasures. Usk itself is an old market town, situated on the river and overlooked by the ruins of a castle which was founded by the de Clare family as a Marcher lord's stronghold in the 12th century. The de Clares built a small square keep with earthworks. In the 13th century the outer bailey and gatehouse were added, and later that century the large round tower was constructed. During the 15th century, other buildings were added to the outer ward. The castle supported the royalists during the civil war and was subsequently dismantled.

Beneath the town are the remains of an old Roman settlement called Burrium. The church of St Mary's was once attached to a Benedictine priory of nuns and dates back to the 13th century. Inside there is a notable Tudor screen, which was restored in 1899, and a 17th-century pulpit. The nave is of decorated style, and the porches perpendicular. A 13th-century gabled priory gateway stands near the churchyard. Cefntilla Court, built in 1616 and restored in 1856, lies two and a half miles north-east of Usk and contains fine pictures and pieces of porcelain. The town is a good touring centre, yet another attraction being Raglan Castle, five miles to the north-east.

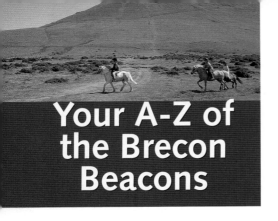

Your A-Z of the Brecon Beacons

Brecon

Having escaped the destructive development that many other towns have suffered, the historic cathedral town of Brecon is now undergoing change. A £4 million shopping arcade opened in August 1996, and a new theatre and arts centre has recently been completed.

Brecon derives its name from that of Brychan, a legendary Welsh Prince. Its illustrious past is disclosed in buildings which remain from previous centuries although much evidence of the town's past lies buried under present-day buildings. Prominent amongst the ancient edifices are the castle, the cathedral – a Benedictine priory of Norman foundation – and a school, Christ College, founded by Henry VIII in 1541 utilising the buildings of a Dominican friary.

The old province of Brycheiniog was taken by force during the last few years of the 11th century by Bernard of Neufmarche, a follower of William the Conqueror in the latter part of his reign. Bernard built the castle which formed a base from which he was able to subdue the three cantreds or regions of the province. The remains of the castle seen today are fragments from the 12th and 13th centuries and include the Ely Tower named after John Mason, Bishop of Ely, who was imprisoned there during the reign of Richard III. The castle was

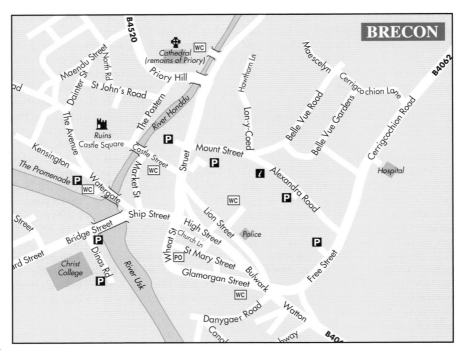

AMGUEDDFA BRYCHEINIOG

Rhodfa'r Capten, Aberhonddu

BRECKNOCK MUSEUM

Captain's Walk, Brecon

Gweithio a Byw o'r Tir	Working & Living off the Land
Labrwyr a Boneddigion yn y Trefi	Journeymen & Gentry in the Towns
Brawdlys o Oes Fictoria	Victorian Assize Court
Darganfyddiadau Celtaidd a Rhufeinig	Celtic & Roman Finds
Ffilm a Lluniau Rhyngweithiol	Interactive Film & Photographs
Sioeau Celf Cyfoes	Contemporary Art Shows
Astudfa Bywyd Gwyllt a Naturiaethwr	Wildlife & Naturalist's Study
Llwyau Caru	Lovespoons
Siop Lyfrau ac Anrhegion	Book & Gift Shop

Llun - Gwener, 10-5	**Mon - Fri, 10-5**
Sadwrn, 10-1, 2-5 (4, Tach-Chwef)	**Sat, 10-1, 2-5 (4, Nov - Feb)**
Dydd Sul, 12-5 (Ebrill-Medi)	**Sun, 12-5 (April - Sept)**
Ar gau dydd Gwener y Groglith;	**Closed Good Friday, Christmas,**
Dydd Nadolig, Gwyl San Steffan	**Boxing Day & New Year's Day**
a Dydd Calan	

Ffôn/Tel: 01874 624121 **Powys** **Facs/Fax: 01874 611281**

Theatr Brycheiniog, Brecon

With the support of the Welsh Office and the Arts Council of Wales Lottery Scheme, Theatr Brycheiniog, a stunning centre for the arts and entertainment has been built in front of the delightful new canal basin just a few minutes' walk from Brecon town centre.

The theatre is open every day to visitors with an excellent canal side bistro and bar, a gallery with changing exhibitions and an exciting programme of events all year round. The theatre is host to Britain's best entertainers, with productions by national touring theatre companies as well as leading orchestras, dance companies, television celebrities and West End shows. There are also plenty of opportunities to enjoy a wealth of local talent with performances by local dramatic and musical societies, choirs and youth groups.

The theatre has been designed with the emphasis on access for all with level access and lifts to all public areas, spaces for patrons in wheelchairs in the stalls and balcony, tactile signage, an infra-red system for the hard of hearing, reserved car parking for disabled patrons and adapted toilets.

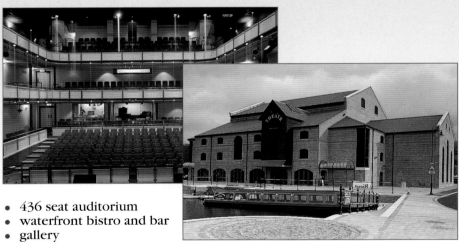

- 436 seat auditorium
- waterfront bistro and bar
- gallery
- studio space
- drama • dance • music • comedy
- children's shows • community events

Box Office - Information 01874 611622
Theatr Brycheiniog, Canal Wharf, Brecon LD3 7EW

Brycheiniog

garrisoned for the king during the Civil War by Sir Herbert Price.

Above the town on the Priory Hill stands the cathedral church of St John the Evangelist, mother church of the Diocese of Swansea & Brecon created in 1923, a fine structure dating from the 13th century. A priory was established on this site by Roger, a monk of the Benedictine monastery of St Martin at Battle, Sussex, and confessor to Bernard of Neufmarche. Little now remains of the original abbey except the font. The cathedral is cruciform in plan and has an early English tower and chancel and a 14th-century nave in the decorated style. In the 15th century the priory was a noted place of pilgrimage. The Welsh bards wrote in praise of a magnificent golden rood in the church which was believed to have miraculous powers. The original 18th-century ring of six bells, last rung in 1803 when Lord Nelson passed through the town, was replaced in 1995. The new peal of ten bells includes three of the original bells cast by Abel Rudhall of Gloucester in 1745.

After the dissolution of the priory in 1537, Henry VIII gave the priory buildings to Sir John Price, an eminent local scholar and gentleman. These buildings, surrounded by the medieval priory wall, were returned to the church at the time it was elevated to the status of cathedral and much has been done to restore these buildings to ecclesiastical use.

A superb new Heritage Centre now stands within the beautiful medieval Cathedral Close. The renovated 16th-century tythe barn, with its mullioned windows, contains an exhibition depicting the development of the priory and cathedral, and a cathedral shop. There is also a licensed restaurant, within the Cathedral Close.

The parish church of St. Mary is basically a medieval building on a Norman

foundation, but the tower dates from the 16th century.

The remains of Brecon Castle lie partly in the grounds of the Castle Hotel and partly in the bishop's garden. The ruins are fragments from the 12th and 13th centuries, and remains of the medieval town walls can be seen in several areas. Brecon also has some fine Georgian and Jacobean town houses.

On the other bank of the River Usk, which is spanned by an ancient bridge, is the site of Christ College. This was founded in 1541 and became a public school in 1860.

The town is the home of the South Wales Borderers – famed for their courageous defence of Rorke's Drift against overwhelming odds in the Zulu War – and their early 19th-century barracks include a military museum. The county museum is in Glamorgan Street.

Brecon itself is a market town with a

good shopping centre and excellent car parking facilities. There are ample opportunities for sports, including a swimming pool, a tennis court, bowling greens, two golf courses – all within easy reach - and pony trekking and riding centres.

Beautiful countryside surrounds Brecon, and the Brecon Beacons are virtually on the doorstep, rising nearly 3,000 feet to provide a dramatic backdrop.

Brecknock Museum & Gallery This is one of the most charming and attractive museums in Wales, and a visit is strongly recommended. The displays are beautifully presented and include Celtic crosses, a famous Dark Age canoe discovered in nearby Llangorse Lake and a Victorian assize court. You can see an 1880's court case re-enacted in the assize court. You will also see one of Wales' finest collections of lovespoons, along with exhibits focusing on prehistory and natural history. A new attraction is the stunning Brecknock Townlife gallery, This

Brecon

Brecon Cathedral

has doubled the number of exhibits and
includes an interactive data bank of old
photographs and film clips which are
projected on to a large screen. The museum's
art gallery also stages one of the liveliest
exhibition programmes of Welsh art to be
found anywhere in the principality. For
further information ring 01874 624121.

Theatr Brycheiniog, Brecon For further
information ring 01874 611622.

Coliseum Film Centre, Brecon For
further information ring 01874 622501.

Jazz Aberhonddu/Brecon Jazz Festival
Brecon has always been known for its
spectacular natural beauty - and for over a
decade it has also achieved world-wide fame
for its annual jazz festival.

This incongruous juxtaposition of Welsh
mountain scenery and jazz has produced an
explosive atmosphere of sound and
celebration which attracts visitors from all

over Britain and beyond. They come for concerts given by the world's greatest jazz musicians, and for the extraordinary carnival feeling more synonymous with the Mediterranean than a small market town in Mid Wales.

During one glorious August weekend, Brecon plays host to about 100 concerts and 50,000 people. Venues, both indoors and in the open air, are spread throughout the town, so that the audience is constantly on the move from one style of music to the next. Coloured canopies stretch between the Georgian buildings, and the music ranges from marching bands to artists of the calibre of Benny Carter, Sonny Rollins, Gerry Milligan and Stephane Grappelli to the younger lions of today - Wynton Marsalis, Pat Metheny and Michel Petrucciani.

In 1996 Brecon Jazz added another string to its bow by opening the world's first Jazz Gallery. "This welcome new attraction" (as *The Times* described it) houses a marvellously original audio-visual exhibition

Brecon

telling the story of jazz, from its beginnings in the rhythms of West Africa and via the slave trade and the Mississippi riverboats to the European festivals of today. It is a unique gallery, also displaying paintings and photographs by artists who work at the festival, and is open all year round. Arrangements can be made for visits by school parties. For more information about the festival or new jazz gallery and information centre, ring Brecon Jazz on 01874 625557.

Riding in the Brecon Beacons

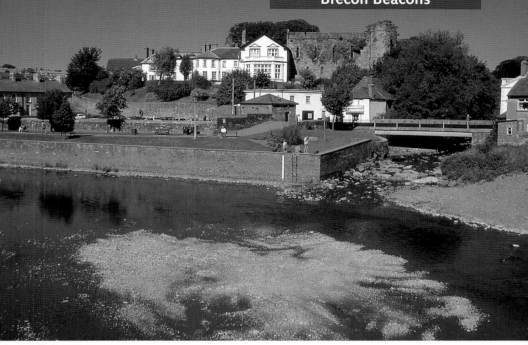

Overlooking Brecon

The South Wales Borderers and Monmouthshire Regiment Museum The museum spans 280 years of military history and houses a large Zulu War display featuring the heroic defence of Rorke's Drift. Exhibits include armoury, medals, uniforms and paintings. For further information ring 01874 613310.

Bronllys

The local church has a detached tower. In times of trouble women and children were sent to the upper floor, while the cattle were kept safely in the lower part. The nearby 12th-century Bronllys Castle is one and a half miles south on the A479 Talgarth to Bronllys road.

Bwlch

A small village affording beautiful views as the A40 climbs up to it from Abergavenny to Brecon, Bwlch lies four miles south-east of Llangorse Lake and is within the national park. Further views of the Brecon Beacons

61

open up to the south, beyond the village.

Capel-y-Ffin

Capel-y-Ffin is a small hamlet near the head of the Llanthony valley, in the Black Mountains. A neo-Benedictine community was founded here in 1869 and they built the monastery and a church named Llanthony Abbey. The picturesque little white church, distinctive for its drunken bell-turret, is worth a visit.

Craig-y-Nos

A former palatial home of the Victorian prima donna Adelina Patti, Craig-y-Nos is located off the A4067 in the Tawe valley 4½ miles north of Ystradgynlais. The house is not open to visitors, but 40 acres of grounds which were acquired as a country park by the National Park Authority in 1976 offer pleasant walks through woodlands and meadows.

Crickhowell

Crickhowell

This pleasant little town nestles beneath Pen Cerrig-Calch mountain (2,302 feet), on the main road between Abergavenny and Brecon, in one of the most beautiful sections of the valley of the Usk. The river winds through rich parklands and under the old thirteen-arched bridge, which is the chief architectural glory of Crickhowell. Strongly buttressed, the bridge was built in the 17th century. It displays segmented arches with double-arch rings built in two orders, with the stones forming the outer ring smaller than those in the inner ring. Two of the arches have been rebuilt. and the bridge, which has a total span of 140 yards, has been widened on the upstream side.

Sadly, Crickhowell Castle is in a much sorrier state. It was built towards the end of the 11th century and all that remains are the motte and bailey, parts of the wall, and a small round tower. Owain Glyndwr stormed and destroyed most of the castle in 1403.

Three quarters of a mile west of the town is Gwern Vale House, where Sir George Everest was born in 1790. Mount Everest was named after this great military engineer, who did much of his surveying in India. He is buried in the churchyard at Crickhowell. Also west of the town is the 14th century gatehouse at Porthmawr, which has survived a now-vanished Tudor mansion that belonged to the Herbert family. The Craig-y-Cilau nature reserve lies two miles southwest of the town. The Welsh Brigade Museum is close to Crickhowell at Cwrt-y-Gollen Camp.

Along the foot of the hills runs the

Coffee Shop
Take-away Service
Sandwiches - Plain.
Toasted.
Jacket Pots Various
Fillings .
Pasties
Quiche .
Salads.
Homemade. Cakes.

At Rear.

Crickhowell — The cheese press

Monmouthshire and Brecon Canal – one of
the most delightful holiday waterways in the
whole of Britain and navigable from
Pontypool to Brecon itself. It offers an
unrivalled series of locks, towpaths, tunnels
and swing bridges in splendid scenery all the
way along the Usk valley. Narrow roads twist
northwards from Crickhowell into the
slender valley of the Grwyne Fechan, which
curves around the back of the Sugar Loaf.
Here is the little village of Llanbedr Ystrad
Yw, with its ancient church and air of
complete peace. The Grwyne Fechan is a
walking and riding region, for it is a dead end
for motorists. The Grwyne Fawr and the
smaller stream join at Llanbedr: again a
valley with no drivable road out of it at the
top end, which is guarded by a small
reservoir. The two Grwyne valleys show the
Black Mountains at their best, and the
Grwyne Fawr has the tiny church of
Partrishow, with its early Tudor rood screen,
decorated with Welsh dragons, wall murals
with the figure of Death, and an oaken roof.
There are beautiful views from the
churchyard.

Crickhowell Castle The site is open to
visitors.

Nantyffin Cider Mill A mile and a half
west of Crickhowell, in a beautiful setting
overlooking the Usk, this acclaimed bar and
restaurant has been converted from a 16th-
century cider mill. It attracts many visitors
appreciative of fine food in charming
surroundings - and probably none more
famous than ex-U.S. president Jimmy Carter,
who dined here in August 1996.

Cwmyoy

A hamlet in the Black Mountains' Vale of
Ewyas, 4 miles south of Llanthony, Cwmyoy
is noted for possessing the 'crookedest
church in Wales' – a strictly architectural
reference, as the tower and nave are askew.

Defynnog

The village church, with its 15th-century
tower, was formerly the centre of a large
parish, and it houses a 12th-century font
which bears the only Runic inscription in
Wales. Defynnog lies nine miles west of
Brecon and in the 19th century was
important for its cattle and sheep markets.

Hay-on-Wye

This charming market town, situated at
the north-east corner of the Brecon Beacons

Hay-on-Wye

National Park, is famous for its proliferation of second-hand bookshops. It is the gateway to the Welsh section of the Wye Valley, and is a typical border town. The Hay Bluff (2,219 feet) and Lord Hereford's Knob (2,263 feet) rise from the Black Mountains in the south.

At one time the town was a centre for the flannel industry, but it is now a local farming focus, where Clun and Kerry sheep are sold at the market. In the older part of the town the streets contain numerous little shops and are narrow and winding. The parish Church of St Mary dates largely from 1834, when it was rebuilt and enlarged. It still includes the early English southern entrance and 13th-century lower part of the square tower.

The first castle built here was a motte-and-bailey structure probably erected by a Norman knight called Revell in the 11th century. Traces of this can be found near the church, and the walk past here is known as Bailey Walk. A fine gateway, the keep, and parts of the walls are all that remain.

Alongside this ruin is a privately-owned, early 17th-century Jacobean house which replaced the castle. The town itself has been described as a book-buyer's paradise. There are bookshops everywhere, hence it earned the reputation for itself as the second-hand book capital of the world. Other interesting shops, include those selling arts and crafts.

A spectacular mountain road south from Hay climbs to the 1,778 feet summit of the Gospel Pass in the Black Mountains before dropping down into the secluded Vale of Ewyas, Capel-y-ffin and Llanthony. A few miles west of Hay, just off the A438, is Maesyronnen Chapel, which is believed to be the first in Wales. The stone long house, built in about 1696 and still filled with wooden furniture from the 18th and 19th centuries, was originally a secret meeting place of nonconformist dissenters. The churchyard at nearby Llowes contains a fine Celtic cross.

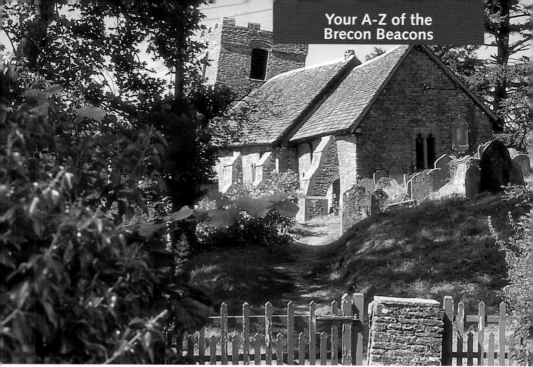

Cwmyoy

Libanus

Situated on the A470 south-west of Brecon, this hamlet gives access to the Brecon Beacons Mountain Centre. Close by is the National Trust's Blaenglyn Farm.

Llanddeusant

Located in the foothills of the Black Mountain, this hamlet is a popular starting point for a visit to the lake of Llyn y Fan Fach, source of the Sawdde river.

Llanddew

Llanddew is a hamlet three miles north-east of Brecon. Apart from the unusual cruciform church, Llanddew's main claim to fame is the remarkable site of the former Bishop's Palace in which Archdeacon of Brecon – Giraldus Cambrensis, or Gerald of Wales – resided for twenty-five years and wrote his well-known Itinerary Through Wales. Only a few ruined walls of the palace remain today.

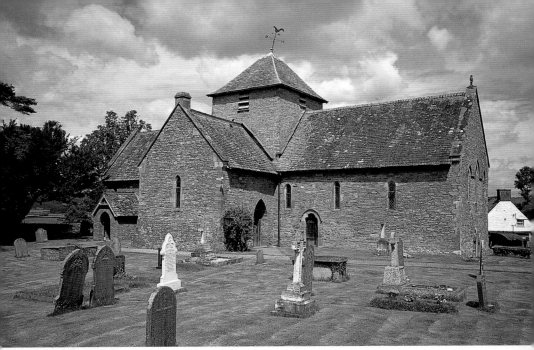

Llanddew Church

Llanelieu

This village lies two miles east of Talgarth and has a remote little Anglican church with a 14th-century rood-screen and 7th- and 9th-century pillar stones. The village is also known for Llanelieu Court, which is said to have originated as a 14th-century monastic cell of Llanthony Priory.

Llanfilo

This hamlet is situated about two miles west of Talgarth. The little church, among the most attractive in the area, features lovely oak pews, altar rails and pulpit dating from the 17th century, and rood-loft and screen from c1500. The porch and timbered roof date from 1350 and the font is pre-Norman.

Llangorse Lake & Village

Llangorse Lake (Llyn Syfaddan), five miles south-east of Brecon, is the largest natural lake in South Wales and the second largest in the principality. It lies in a very attractive setting with hills and mountains on

three sides. The lake is about two miles long, half a mile wide and has a shoreline of nearly four miles. On its east side rise the west flanks of the Black Mountains – the conical summit of Mynydd Troed (1,997 feet) and the flat-topped Mynydd Llangorse (1,661 feet). To the south-east, the slopes of Mynydd Llangorse drop down to the 650 feet-high pass at Bwlch, which leads to the Usk valley. Buckland Hill rises to 1,038 feet west of Bwlch, and is half hidden by Allt yr Esgair (1,250 feet) – the wooded hill south of the lake. To the west and north-west the hills are lower, but the scene to the south-west is dominated by the Brecon Beacons, with the high ridge from Craig Pwllfa (2,504 feet) leading west to Cribin (2,608 feet) and the main summits of Pen-y-fan (2,906 feet) and Corn-du (2,863 feet).

Llangorse is a pleasant village situated close to the lake and has a 14th-century church with a small tower. Although heavily restored in the last century, the building retains a good 15th-century wagon roof, a wide south aisle with an arcade of four bays,

LICENSED TO CARRY 5 30?

Llangorse Lake

and an ancient inscribed stone. To the west is Llanfihangel Tal-y-llyn, and a road leads to the shore. The small church here carries a medieval tower and was restored in 1870. On the south shore almost opposite Llangorse is the church and scattered hamlet of Llangasty Talyllyn. The church, situated right on the water's edge, was built in 1849 for a relative of Robert Raikes, the pioneer of Sunday schools in the late 18th century. It has many interesting modern interior details, and the tower offers a good viewpoint. To the south-west is Treberfedd, a mansion built in Tudor style for the Raikes family, descendants of Robert.

Llangynidr

Situated halfway between Abergavenny and Brecon, this small village lies in one of the most attractive stretches of the Usk valley. To the north of the river are Buckland Hill (1,038 feet) and Myarth, with the lower

Llyn-y-Fan Fach

slopes of Mynydd Llangorse (1,600 feet) visible between them above the village of Bwlch. On the south side are Mynydd Llangynidr and Mynydd Llangattock, both over 1,700 feet high, with the conical peak of Tor-y-Foel (1,806 feet) overlooking the Dyffryn Crawnan to the west. The B4560 from Llangynidr to Beaufort makes a winding ascent over Mynydd Llangattock, reaching a summit viewpoint of 1,694 feet. The panorama from the top includes the Usk valley and many of the summits of the Black Mountains, including Mynydd Llangorse, Pen Allt-mawr, Pen Cerrig-Calch, Crug Mawr, and the Sugar Loaf.

Llangynidr has a picturesque old bridge over the River Usk, dating from c1600, which has six arches and massive cutwaters. Attractive walks along the river extend in both directions from the south side. Between the Usk and the main part of the village lies the Monmouthshire and Brecon Canal, now in use for pleasure craft. Nearly one mile east of the village, on the B4558 Crickhowell road and situated across the canal, is Aberhoyw – an attractive farmhouse with a coat of arms dated 1726. Nearby is the modern house of Worcester Lodge, situated in a fine position by the river almost opposite Gliffaes, an Italianate mansion with a beautiful garden containing rare shrubs and trees.

Llanthony

This hamlet is located in the Llanthony valley in the Black Mountains, and its popular tourist attraction is the 12th century ruins of Llanthony Priory, founded by Norman Marcher Lord Walter de Lacy as an Augustinian monastery. The site offers good hill walking on the ridges of the Black Mountains.

Llyn-y-Fan Fach & Llyn-y-Fan Fawr

These two remote lakes can only be reached on foot, either from the minor road from Trecastle to Glyntawe, or by a more arduous trudge below the Black Mountain's scarp. Llyn-y-Fan Fawr is even more remote than Llyn-y-Fan Fach; this lake lies at the foot of the Fan Hir ridge of the Black Mountain, and at 1,950 feet is the highest in the park.

Llyswen

This attractive village is situated next the River Wye and has won the Best Kept Village award in Powys for the last ten years. The village was visited by Wordsworth in the 1800's. The village has a pretty church which dates back to 1660.

Myddfai

This village is reached by any of numerous lanes from Llandovery and is associated with Llyn-y-Fan Fach's 'Lady of the Lake' legend. A memorial to the legend and the 'Physicians of Myddfai' can be found in the church porch.

Partrishow

The small hamlet of Partrishow can be found in the quiet lanes and hills above Abergavenny. The tiny but pretty church contains an exceptional rood screen, one of the finest in Wales. The delicate, very elaborate screen, carved in oak, was the work of highly-skilled Tudor craftsmen. The isolated church evokes a strong sense of times past. It dates from the 11th century and features a Norman font and macabre wall painting of a skeleton depicting death.

A cul-de-sac from the church to the north leads through the forested slopes of the remote Grwyne Fawr valley.

Sennybridge

Situated where the River Senni flows into the River Usk about eight miles west of Brecon, Sennybridge lies on the north edge of the Brecon Beacons National Park. It is an important centre for the marketing of sheep and cattle for the surrounding area. Castell Du, now a ruin, stands on the west bank of the Senni and is believed to have been constructed during the 13th century. It comprises a small round keep with a smaller building attached, and at one time was used as a prison by the keepers of Fforest Fawr.

Glynderi Pottery Take the turning at Sennybridge towards Pentrefelin, and just after crossing the Llwyncyntefin Bridge over the River Usk you will discover Glynderi Pottery, attractively located within the coachhouse of a 17th-century Welsh longhouse.

Ruth Lyle makes beautiful stoneware pots here. Attractive ranges of domestic wares are displayed in the large gallery alongside one-off pots, bells, frog mugs and an exciting range of slip-trailed decorated sheep pots. There are also carefully selected gifts, such as jewellery and glass.

Visitors are welcome to browse and watch any work in progress, such as preparing clay, throwing and glazing. Children are encouraged to model clay in a free activity area set aside for them. The pottery is open all year. For further information ring 01874 636564.

Skenfrith

Situated close to the English border about eight miles north-west of Monmouth, this village stands beside the River Monnow. The river is excellent for trout fishing. Skenfrith's 13th-century castle is one of three forming a triangle of defence, the others being Grosmont and White. Ruins include a round tower enclosed by a four-sided curtain wall and a moat. The wall probably had five towers, but only four remain. It ceased to be of importance after the end of the Welsh uprisings, and was probably in ruins by the 16th century. The castle is now owned by the National Trust. The local church also dates back to the 13th

century and has an impressive, partially-timbered tower.

Storey Arms

Storey Arms lies in the heart of the Brecon Beacons National Park. It is at the top of a pass (1440 feet) through the mountains and close to the highest peaks in South Wales. Pont ar Daf at Storey Arms is the place from where most people set off to walk to the Beacons' distinctive, flat-topped summit of Pen y Fan (2,907 feet). There are a number of different paths to the summit, and it is advisable to make reference to an Ordnance Survey map to get away from the main paths which become very busy during the spring and summer seasons.

There is a car park and Outdoor Education Centre at the site. Storey Arms is also a Mountain Rescue Post.

Talgarth

This small market town is set at the foot of the Black Mountains. Talgarth lies in the

Brecon Beacons National Park and to the south-east rise the lofty peaks of Waun Fach (2,660 feet) and Pen-y-Gader (2,624 feet). Eight cattle markets were once held here annually. The church is dedicated to St. Gwendoline and dates from the 13th century. It was restored in 1873. The south aisle displays an excellent 14th-century sepulchral slab. A square 14th-century pele tower standing at the east end of a local bridge was once used as a lookout post, but has since been converted into a house.

Hywel Harris, a founder of Methodism in Wales, came from the village. He intended to enter the Church of England, but after he was refused ordination on three occasions he became a wandering preacher. Later in life he set up a communal farming centre at nearby Trefecca, where the inhabitants lived an almost monastic life. He was supported in this venture by the Countess of Huntingdon. After his death in 1773 and subsequent burial in Talgarth churchyard, a chapel was erected at Trefecca to his memory.

Bronllys Castle For more details contact the local Tourist Information Centre on 01874 622485.

Hywel Harris Museum For more information ring 01874 711423.

Talgarth Festival of the Black Mountains. Organised each year by the Talgath Trust - established as a result of the formation of the Talgarth Action Group For more information ring 01874 711382.

Talybont
This village is situated on the Monmouthshire-Brecon canal in the Usk valley. The town provides a good centre for exploring the canal, either on the towpath or by boat. The large Talybont Reservoir is a couple of miles to the south. The reservoir is one of many set in the Brecon Beacons and

Brecon Beacons

Acquired by the Taylors in 1998 and completely refurbished to meet its new role as a Country Inn & Restaurant with rooms of excellence.

- Bar with log fire
- Real Ales
- Choice of wines by the glass or bottle
- Lots of board games
- Garden & Patio
- Children very welcome
- All rooms en suite
- Chef Proprietor using fresh local produce in:
- Restaurant &
- Food served in bar & garden
- Open all day 7 days a week

WTB 3 STAR · RAC ACCLAIMED

tel. (44) 1874 676251

THE USK INN TALYBONT

Station Rd., Talybont on Usk, Brecon, Powys LD3 7JE

built to serve industrial South Wales. This particular one takes its name from Talybont-on-Usk – which lies to the north – and serves the town of Newport. It is situated in a wooded valley and provides a wonderful refuge for wild fowl.

Trecastle

This village is situated on the A40, about 10 miles west of Brecon, and was once a notable stage for a change of horses on the Gloucester-Llandovery mail and stage coach route. In Norman times the Lord of Brecon had an outpost here: the remaining tree-clad motte and bailey castle is the largest in the national park, but only the mound and other earthworks are to be seen today.

Trefecca

This hamlet is about one mile south-west of Talgarth and is noted for its Trefecca College theological study centre. This is the site of the community set up by Hywel Harris in 1752, and the residence he erected is still occupied by the college, together with modern additions. On the outskirts of the village there is the 16th-century College Farm where in 1768 Harris's supporter, the Countess of Huntingdon, established an academy for Methodist preachers.

Tretower

Tretower is a small village situated on the A429 about two and a half miles north of Crickhowell. Lying beside the Rhiangoll stream are the remains of a 13th-century Norman castle and a fortified mansion of the 14th and 15th centuries. The land was granted to the Norman knight Picard by the Lord of Brecon, and he constructed a motte surrounded by a polygonal stone wall. After the Welsh had managed to capture it for a short while in 1233, the English strengthened it by building a tall circular

Llangynidr

keep inside the wall. To this they added three round towers. It was later rebuilt and turned into one of the finest early fortified mansions in Wales. It is built round a courtyard and has an impressive gatehouse. After 1777 the court became a farmhouse and by 1936 had fallen into disrepair. Extensive repairs to restore it to its former glory have recently been carried out. Both castle and court are open to visitors. The main room is a large 15th-century banqueting hall, and overlooking the courtyard is a gallery dating from the 14th century. The mystical poet Henry Vaughan lived here during the 17th century.

Tretower Court & Castle This is open all year round. For more information ring 01874 730279.

Llyn y Fan Fawr

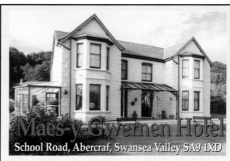
Ystradfellte

This hamlet in the upper Mellte valley is located near the border of the Brecon Beacons National Park. The landscape here is very different from the open mountainside of other areas of the park, with wooded gauges, waterfalls, caves and potholes. The geology also changes here, from Carboniferous limestone to Old Red Sandstone – the rock from which the main bulk of the Beacons is formed.

Ystradgynlais

Ystradgynlais is a Tawe valley town lying on the border of the Brecon Beacons to the north and the industrial towns to the south. St. Mary's parish church dates from 1648. Further up the valley are fine examples of limestone scenery, and on the other side of the valley the Ffynnon Ddu (Black Spring) water gushes forth from a remarkable cave system.

PARC CENEDLAETHOL BANNAU BRYCHEINIOG

**BRECON BEACONS
NATIONAL
PARK**

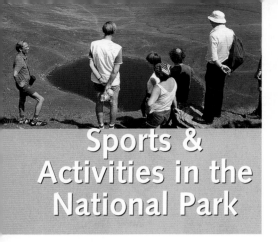

Sports & Activities in the National Park

The Brecon Beacons are one of the finest outdoor playgrounds in southern Britain. The mix of spectacular highland scenery, beautiful river valleys, forested hillsides, sun-dappled lakes and rushing rivers means that you'll never be short of outdoor action here.

The area has long been a magnet for walkers - with magnificent views across much of South Wales from the summit of peaks such as Pen-y-Fan it's little surprise that there's barely a day of the year when the more popular paths aren't being trodden by someone. And if you like to stroll rather than hike, the area's valleys and woodlands provide some beautiful gentle walking.

Elsewhere rock climbing and abseiling can get the adrenalin pumping, and if this doesn't give you enough altitude how about paragliding or gliding? Talgarth is one of Britain's top sites for both sports.

Back on the ground mountain biking is a popular activity, with some superb trails over the hills and through the forests, and the less-demanding Taff Trail, which is part of the Welsh National Cycle Route (Lon Las Cymru) is popular with family groups. Road cyclists will also find that the National Cycle Route can direct you through some beautiful - and challenging - scenery (try the ride over Gospel Pass between Hay-on-Wye and Abergavenny for instance!). Horse riding and pony trekking have been well-established in the area since the 1950's, and are a great way to discover the fantastic scenery of the area on the extensive network of bridleways, whether on a trek of a few hours or a few days.

The action also continues underground, as there are some of the country's top caving sites within the Beacons, such as Llangattock Mountain near Crickhowell. And the rivers, canals and lakes of the Beacons are superb for canoeing, with water to suit everyone from white water expert to complete beginner. Llangorse Lake is also popular as a windsurfing site.

What follows is a brief guide to the various centres which can help you get out and explore the great outdoors. For more experienced types looking to find their own action there are plenty of local guide books to every sport from mountain biking to caving - or you can just get out there and discover it all for yourself!

Canoeing

Wye Valley Canoe Centre Established in 1968 and located at Glasbury in the beautiful Wye Valley, the Centre offers canoe hire and tuition to suit all grades and abilities. And you can take advantage of 100 miles of gently-flowing river. For more information ring 01497 847213.

Climbing

Llangorse Rope Centre A large indoor climbing and activity centre, open all year. Climbing is on natural rock or man-made walls, bouldering, children's walls, abseiling, log climb, rope climb, rope bridges, cave and zip wire. For more information and bookings call 01874 658272/584

Gliding

Black Mountains Gliding Club Talgarth is the UK's premier ridge, wave and

thermal soaring site. The airfield location provides more and stronger soaring conditions all year round than any other gliding site in the British Isles. Flying usually takes place only when it is possible to soar, and in 1990 the club flew and soared 285 out of the 364 days available. On average the two-seater flight time is 45 minutes, allowing beginners much more flying time and therefore faster learning progress than is normal at the average gliding site. Beginners can normally expect two flights or more a day, up to an hour in duration, depending on prevailing conditions and availability.

A fixed fee is charged for the course, and flying is charged in two parts – the launch and soaring time. Holiday courses are normally run Monday to Friday all year round. The number of pilots on a course is limited to four per instructor to ensure maximum individual attention and the best utilisation of soaring conditions. The club operates two to three two-seater sailplanes – K13, Blanik, IS30 and IS32 plus one single-seat SZD 51-1 Junior. Launch is by 235 hp PA25 Piper Pawnee. All instructors are highly experienced. For further information ring 01874 711463 or 711254.

Golf

Brecon Golf Club For more information ring 01874 622004.

Cradoc Golf Club This picturesque 18-hole parkland course was designed by C.K. Cotton in 1969. Situated two miles north of Brecon, off the B4520, the club offers full catering and bar facilities and welcomes visitors. For further information ring 01874 623658.

Horse Riding

Llangorse Riding Centre Overlooking Llangorse Lake, this fully-approved centre offers trekking, riding and hacking for all abilities. Many pleasant routes with fantastic views follow paths through farmland and open hills adjoining the centre. Accommodation can be arranged locally. For further information and bookings call 01874 658272/584

Tregoyd Riding Centre Located in the national park 3 miles from Hay-on-Wye, this centre welcomes beginners and experienced riders of all ages and offers horse riding, pony trekking and trail riding. You can also book a riding holiday here, with accommodation arranged locally. For more information ring 01497 847351, or fax 01497 847680.

Leisure Centres & Swimming Pools

Brecon Leisure Centre This superb new Centre in the heart of Brecon is open 7 days a week, all year round. Facilities include swimming pools, flume, sports halls, health and fitness suites, 10-pin and indoor green bowling, climbing walls, athletics track, playing fields, creche and a comprehensive activities programme. For more information ring 01874 623677.

Crickhowell Sports Centre For more information ring 01873 810997.

Gwernyfed Sports Centre, near Brecon Located at Three Cocks, the Centre has a wide range of indoor and outdoor activities. Facilities include multi-purpose sports hall, fitness suite, tennis courts and playing fields. For more information ring 01874 847740.

Hay-on-Wye Swimming Pool Suitable for beginners, intermediates and most watersports, it can be booked for special events. For more information ring 01497 820431.

Sennybridge Sports Centre For more information ring 01874 636512.

Ystradgynlais Sports Centre Located to the south of Ystradgynlais, the Centre is open all through school holidays and at weekends, and in the evenings during term time. Facilities include 25-metre swimming pool, extensive fitness suite, sunbed, sports hall, aerobics, aqua aerobics and circuits. For more information ring 01639 844854.

Outdoor Pursuits

Black Mountain Activities The Centre, based in Glasbury-on-Wye, was set up in the early 1990's by outdoor pursuit instructors Carl and Hugh Durham, who have a wealth of experience in mountaineering, canoeing and caving. The Centre is approved by the British Canoe Union and accredited by Wales Tourist Board. All staff hold the relevant national qualification of the pursuit in which they lead. Black Mountain's clients come from all over the British Isles, ranging from individuals, schools, youth and social groups to large blue chip British companies. Courses are individually designed for each group, from a single activity on a specialist course to a multi-activity week. For further information ring 01497 847897.

Crickhowell Adventure Gear With stores in Crickhowell, Brecon and Abergavenny, this is where you will find all the best brands of specialist caving, climbing, lightweight camping and mountaineering equipment, plus outdoor and casual clothing. Local advice on walking and climbing is also available, with courses on canoeing, mountain biking, gorge walking and other pursuits. For more information ring 01873 810020.

Llangorse Rope Centre. From this large indoor climbing centre outdoor activities such as caving, gorge walking or hill walking can be arranged for groups. For more information please ring 01874 658272/584.

Mountain & Water promotes enjoyment of the countryside and great outdoors through a variety of relaxed activities - canoeing, kayaking, rock climbing, abseiling and orienteering among them. Launched in 1987, this unique enterprise offers courses, field studies and other activities led by experienced instructors who share a common love of the Brecon Beacons and its landscape. For further information ring 01873 831825.

Talybont Venture Centre The centre runs a wide range of outdoor group activities and management development courses, including mountain bike hire (helmets, toolkits and routes provided), caving, abseiling, activity days (river crossings etc) and gorge walking.For further details ring 01874 676458.

Cycling in Mid Wales

Cycling is a non-polluting, healthy and fun activity for all the family and with modern bikes offering a wide range of gears and accessories it's an ideal way of enjoying the countryside and wildlife of the Heart of Wales, as well as providing a good alternative to the car for short journeys.

Mid Wales has much to offer leisure cyclists, from quiet country lanes and byways suitable for families and touring, to wild off-road tracks providing exhilarating riding for mountain bikers and trail enthusiasts.

The central section of Lon Las Cymru, the Welsh National Cycle Route from Holyhead to Cardiff, runs through the region and forms a principal route of the rapidly developing National Cycle Network. The route comprises a total of 288 miles of minor roads and traffic-free paths, is fully signed and detailed maps are available from Tourist Information Centres and local cycling outlets, many of which offer cycle hire facilities and guided rides.

In Powys the main route offers a journey through spectacular scenery on quiet country roads and byways which avoids steep gradients as much as possible. For the more adventurous, the route also has an optional westerly section which passes through the wild mountain and forest areas between Machynlleth and Llanwrtyd Wells. There is also an option to follow Route 42 from Hay on Wye to Abergavenny over the spectacular Gospel Pass.

From Brecon south to Cardiff, the route follows the well established Taff Trail providing a mainly off-road cycle and footpath passing many sights of interest and industrial heritage as it passes through the Brecon Beacons and Taff valley. Most of the trail follows easy gradients with the occasional steeper section and is suitable for all ages and abilities.

Cycling through the Gospel Pass in Brecknockshire.

Exploring the Countryside (Copyright Sustrans/Andy Traynor)

In addition to long distance routes, many local route networks are being developed, based around Mid-Wales towns, providing ideal circular day rides to suit all levels. Guides to routes around Brecon, Llanwrtyd Wells, Llanidloes, Presteigne and Knighton are available locally.

Powys County Council is working with many organisations in developing a county-wide cycle network including regional routes of the National Cycle Network, local routes, cycle parking and links to public transport.

Transport for all the family! (Copyright Sustrans/Andy Traynor)

For further information contact:
Cycling Development Officer
Technical Services Department,
Powys County Council,
County Hall,
Llandrindod Wells,
Powys LD1 5LG
Tel: 01597 826605

Powys

The Powys Cycle Network is being part financed by the European Community European Regional Development Fund.

For more information on the Taff Trail send a 1st class SAE to:

Taff Trail Project c/o Groundwork, Merthyr & Rhondda Cynon Taff, Fedw Hir, Llwydcoed, Aberdare CF44 0DX
Tel: 01685 883880

Lon Las Cymru - The Welsh National Cycle Route.

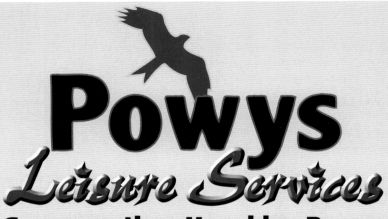

Powys Leisure Services

Gwasanaethau Hamdden Powys

Rhayader Leisure Centre
The ideal venue for Leisure, Parties, Receptions and meetings. Take a dip in our swimming pool. All facilities are available for club or group hire.
Canolfan Hamdden Rhaeadr Dyma fan cyfarfod delfrydol ar gyfer Hamdden, Partion, Derbyniadau a chyfarfodydd. Ewch am drochiad yn y pwll. Mae'r holl gyfleusterau ar gael i'w llogi i grwpiau neu glybiau.
Tel/Rhif ffôn: 01597 811013

Builth Wells Sports Centre Open to the public all day during school holidays and at weekends and evenings in term time. Facilities include multi purpose Sportshall, Fitness and Health Suites and Squash Courts.
Mae **Canolfan Chwaraeon Llanfair-Ym-Muallt** ar agor i'r cyhoedd trwy'r dydd yn ystod y gwyliau ysgol ac ar benwythnosau a nosweithiau yn ystod y tymor ysgol. Mae cyfleusterau yn cynnwys Neuadd Chwaraeon amlbwrpas, Ystafelloedd Ffitrwydd ac lechyd a Chyrtiau Sboncen.
Sports Centre/Y Ganolfan Chwaraeon 01982 552324
Swimming Pool/Y Pwll Nofio 01982 552603

Llanidloes Sports Centre offers the opportunity to improve your leisure activities, whether it be in the acquisition of new skills or to sharpen old ones. This is a chance for the whole family to enjoy the best in sport and recreation.
Mae Canolfan Chwaraeon Llanidloes yn cynnig y cyfle i wella eich gweithgareddau hamdden, un ai drwy gael sgiliau newydd neu i wella a rhoi min ar hen sgiliau. Dyma gyfle i'r teulu i gyd i fwynhau'r gorau mewn chwaraeon a hamdden.
Tel/Rhif ffôn: 01686 412871

The Flash Leisure Centre open 7 days a week facilities include; Leisure Pool with 30 metre flume, rapids ride, jacuzzi, beach area and swim lanes, 80 cover Restaurant, Health Suite with sauna, steam room and sunbeds.
Mae Canolfan Hamdden y Fflash sydd ar agor 7 niwrnod yr wythnos yn meddu ar gyfleusterau sy'n cynnwys; pwll nofio gyda llithren 30 medr, dyfroedd gwyllt, jacwsi, ardal glan y pwll a rhesi nofio, bwyty i ddal 80 o bobl, ystafell iechyd gyda sawna, ystafell stêm a gwelyau haul.
Tel/Rhif ffôn: 01938 555952

Ystradgynlais Sports Centre Facilities include 25m swimming pool, extensive fitness suite, sunbeds, sportshall and a busy activity programme including Aerobics, Aqua Aerobics and Circuits.
Canolfan Chwaraeon Ystradgynlais Mae cyfleusterau yn cynnwys pwll nofio 25 medr, ystafell ffitrwydd mawr, gwelyau haul, neuadd chwaraeon a rhaglen lawn o weithgareddau yn cynnwys Erobeg, Erobeg Aqua a Chylchedau
Tel/Rhif ffôn: 01639 844854

Llandrindod Wells Sports Centre A 20 metre swimming pool is complemented by a large multi purpose sports hall, floodlit playing area and grass pitches. The Centre organises activities such as aerobics and splash dance.
Canolfan Chwaraeon Llandrindod Yn cydfynd â'r pwll nofio, ceir neuadd charwaeon fawr aml-bwrpas, ardal chwarae llifoleuedig a chaeau chwarae glaswellt. Mae'r ganolfan yn trefnu gweithgareddau megis erobeg a dawns sblash.
Tel/Rhif ffôn: 01597 825339/01597 824249

For further details please telephone the Community, Leisure & Recreation Department on
Am fwy o fanylion, ffoniwch yr Adran Gymuned a Hamdden ar

Datblygu Chwaraeon · Sports Development • Cyfleusterau Hamdden · Leisure Facilities

East Radnor Leisure Centre in Presteigne offers a wide range of exciting holiday activities for all the family. There are childrens multi-sport activity sessions, roller discos, soft play adventure and bouncy castle fun! **Mae Canolfan Hamdden Dwyrain Maesyfed** yn Llanandras yn cynnig amrediad eang o weithgareddau gwyliau cyffrous ar gyfer yr holl deulu. Mae yna sesiynau gweithgareddau aml-chwaraeon i blant, disgos ar esgidiau rholio, antur chwarae meddal a hwyl yn y Castell Gwynt!

Tel/Rhif ffôn: 01544 260302

Llanfyllin Sports Centre
We have regular courses and activities for all ages and abilities, all year round. **Canolfan Chwaraeon Llanfyllin** Rydym yn cynnal cyrsiau a gweithgareddau yn rheolaidd ar gyfer pob oedran a gallu trwy gydol y flwyddyn.

Tel/Rhif ffôn: 01691 648814

Caereinion Leisure Centre
The Leisure Centre caters for all the recreational requirements you need, whether its badminton or squash, why not pay a visit? **Canolfan Hamdden Caereinion** Mae'r Ganolfan Hamdden yn darpau ar gyfer eich holl anghenion hamdden, boed yn badminton neu sboncen. Pam na ddewch chi ar ymwcliad?

Tel/Rhif ffôn: 01938 810634

Maldwyn Leisure Centre for all ages and abilities, the centre plays host to numerous local and international events. Whether playing squash or working out in the gym - Maldwyn is the place to be. **Mae Canolfan Hamdden Maldwyn** yn darparu ar gyfer pob oedran a gallu. Mae'r ganolfan wedi croesawu nifer o ddigwyddiadau lleol a rhyngwladol. Boed yn chwarae sboncen neu wneud ymarfer corff yn y gampfa, maldwyn yw'r lle i fod.

Tel/Rhif ffôn: 01686 628771

Hay on Wye Swimming Pool
is a well equipped pool suitable for beginners, intermediates and most water sports. **Mae Pwll Nofio'r Gelli** yn bwll sy'n cynnwys yr holl gyfarpar sy'n addas ar gyfer dechreuwyr, nofwyr o allu canolig ac ar gyfer y mwyafrif o chwaraeon dŵr.

Tel/Rhif ffôn: 01497 820431

Bro Ddyfi Leisure Centre Relax with a swim, sauna and sunbed sessions - or enjoy a game of indoor bowls. A superb Leisure Centre with Mother and Baby Room, access for the Disabled and extensive catering facilities. **Canolfan Hamden Bro Dyfi** Ymlaciwch efo sesiynau nofio, sawna a sesiynau gwely haul-neu mwynhewch gêm o fowls dan do. Canolfan Hamdden Wych gyda Ystafell Mam a'i Phlentyn, mynediad i bobl anabl a chyfleusterau arlwyo helaeth.

Tel/Rhif ffôn: 01654 703300

Brecon Leisure Centre Facilities include Swimming Pools and Flume, Sportshalls, Fitness and Health Suites, Ten Pin and Indoor Green Bowling, Climbing Walls, Athletics Track and Playing Fields. **Canolfan Hamdden Aberhonddu** Mae cyfleusterau yn cynnwys Pyllau Nofio a Llithren, Neuadd Chwaraeon, Ystafell Ffitrwydd ac Iechyd, Bowlio Deg a Lawnt Fowlio Dan Do, Waliau Dringo, Trac Athletau a Meysydd Chwarae.

Tel/Rhif ffôn: 01874 623677

Knighton Leisure Centre Leisure Centre offering a 20 metre swimming pool. It has a fitness suite, squash courts, tennis courts, a fast tanning sunbed, soft play area, 5-a-side, basketball and netball. **Canolfan Hamdden Tref-y-Clawdd** Dyma Ganolfan Hamdden sy'n cynnig pwll nofio 20 medr, ystafell ffitrwydd, cyrtiau tenis, gwely haul sy'n rhoi lliw haul yn gyflym, ardal chwarae meddal, pêl-droed 5 bob ochr, pêl fasged a phêl rwyd.

Tel/Rhif ffôn: 01547 529187

Gwernyfed Sports Centre Facilities include a large multi purpose Sportshall, Fitness Suite, Tennis Courts and Playing Fields. Open to the public Monday to Friday 6pm to 10pm and at weekends on demand. **Canolfan Chwaraeon Gwernyfed** Mae cyfleusterau yn cynnwys Neuadd Chwaraeon aml-bwrpas fawr, Ystafell Ffitrwydd, Cyrtiau Tenis a Meysydd Chwarae. Yn agored i'r cyhoedd o ddydd Llun i ddydd Gwener 6pm i 10pm ac ar benwythnosau yn dibynnu ar alw.

Tel/Rhif ffôn: 01497 847740

Powys *Leisure Services*

01597 826711

Chwarae Plant · Childrens Play • Andoddau Allanol · Outdoor Amenities

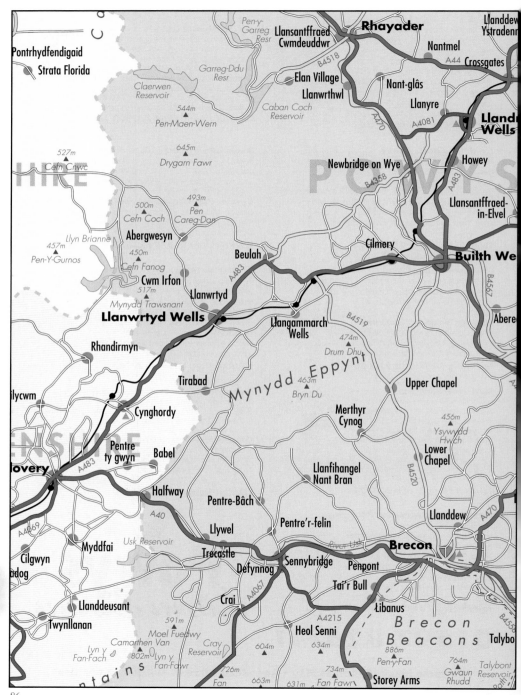

Pontrhydfendigaid
Strata Florida

Pen-y-Garreg Resr
Llansantffraed Cwmdeuddwr
Rhayader
Llanddew Ystradenr

Nantmel
B4518
A44 Crossgates

Claerwen Reservoir
Garreg-Ddu Resr
Elan Village
Llanwrthwl
Nant-glâs

544m
Pen-Maen-Wern
Caban Coch Reservoir
Llanyre
A4081
A470
Lland Wells

527m
Cefn Cnwc
645m
Drygarn Fawr
Newbridge on Wye
B4358
Howey
A483

P O W Y S

HIRE

500m
Cefn Coch
493m
Pen Careg-Dan
Llansantffraed-in-Elvel

Llyn Brianne
450m
Cefn Fanog
Abergwesyn
Beulah
Cilmery
Builth We

457m
Pen-Y-Gurnos
A483
Cwm Irfon
517m
Mynydd Trawsnant
Llanwrtyd
Llanwrtyd Wells
Llangammarch Wells
B4519
Abere
B4567

Rhandirmyn
474m
Drum Dhu

ilycwm
Tirabad
463m
Bryn Du
M y n y d d   E p p y n t
Upper Chapel

Cynghordy
Merthyr Cynog
456m
Ysywydd Hwch

Pentre ty gwyn
Babel
Lower Chapel
B4520

overy
A483
Halfway
Llanfihangel Nant Bran
Llanddew
A470

A40
Pentre-Bâch
Pentre'r-felin
River Usk
Brecon

A4069
Usk Reservoir
Llywel
Sennybridge
Penpont

Cilgwyn
adog
Myddfai
Trecastle
Défynnog
Tai'r Bull
Libanus

Llanddeusant
A4067
Crai
A4215
B r e c o n
B455

Twynllanan
591m
Moel Feuddyr
604m
Heol Senni
634m
B e a c o n s
Talybo

Lyn y Fan-Fach
Camarthen Van
802m
Lyn y Fan-Fawr
Cray Reservoir
886m
Pen-y-Fan
764m
Gwaun Rhudd
Talybont Reservoir

ntains
726m
Fan
663m
631m
Fan Fawr
734m
Storey Arms

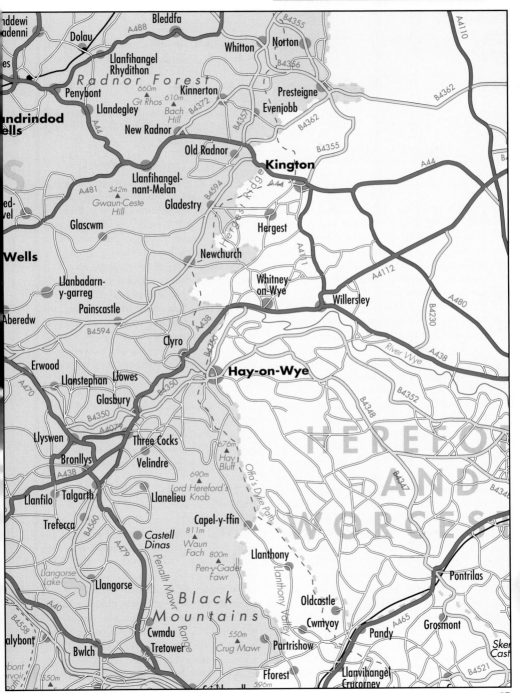

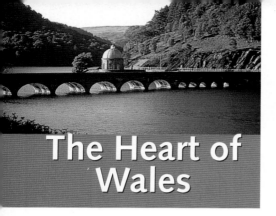

The Heart of Wales

Festival Country

The people of the Brecon Beacons and Mid-Wales clearly know how to enjoy themselves - just take a look at the number of festivals that pop up throughout the year. Hardly a town or village in the area, no matter how small, doesn't have a summer knees-up of some sort.

The theory seems to be that just because we're miles from the metropolis doesn't mean we can't have the best of the city - along with the best of the country - and it works. Few people won't have heard of the world-famous Brecon Jazz Festival, which every August attracts top international stars. Then there's the Royal Welsh Show, one of Britain's most important agricultural events for both farmers and non-farmers.

The Mid Wales Festival of the Countryside is considered by conservationist David Bellamy to be one of the top three sustainable tourism projects in the world, and has events year-round which give you a chance to discover the countryside, rural life and history of Mid-Wales (call 01686 625384 for details).

Then there's Llandrindod Wells' Victorian Festival in August; the Presteigne Festival of Music and Arts, also in August; Builth Wells Festival Week in June; and Knighton May Fair - to name but a few.

And we shouldn't forget Britain's smallest town, Llanwrtyd Wells, which seems to have some sort of shindig every other week - mountain bike and cycling events, walking events, real ale evemnts centred around walking or cycling, the classic man versus horse race, and of course the internationally-famous World Bog Snorkelling Championships!

Full details of the various events and festivals are available from Tourist Information Centres.

The Heart of Wales

The Heart of Wales is, if you'll excuse the pun, a part of the country that has had something of a by-pass as far as visitors are concerned. Yet its landscape of high open hills and impressive crags, deep blue dams and lakes, cascading waterfalls and sparkling rivers, and swathes of forests alternating with lush green valleys, bluebell woods and pastureland beg to be explored.

And dotted amongst all this beauty are an array of charming towns and villages, from tiny hamlets and villages to busy market and spa towns. So here's a quick overview of what the rest of the world has been missing.

Landscape

The most obvious feature of Mid-Wales is its countryside - and the fact that there's so much of it. With just a sprinkling of towns of any real size, you are always within sight and walking distance of unspoilt, inspiring scenery.

In the north of the area lie the imposing 1,600 ft (500 m) whaleback summits of the Cambrian Mountains, close to the market town of Rhayader, with open views across to west Wales, Plynlimon mountain and the southern edges of Snowdonia. The Wye valley runs north and south from Rhayader, and is especially impressive where the river winds its way between steep tumbling crags just north of the town. However, one of the best-known features of this area is man-made, in the form of the series of huge reservoirs of the Elan Valley. Some 70 square miles of hills and valleys was bought by

Llanwrtyd Wells

Birmingham Corporation in 1872 so that the valleys could be flooded to provide the rapidly growing city with water. Eighteen farmhouses, a school and a church disappeared underwater when the valley was flooded, and whilst the ethics of this would be contentious today it's hard to deny that the resulting scenery is anything less than impressive. As, indeed, are the dams. Built with typical Victorian respect for workmanship and a job well done, the dams are impressive monuments to the past - as is the engineering that ensured the water flowed downhill all the way from here to Birmingham! You an learn more about the area and the dams at the Elan Valley Visitor Centre.

To the east of Rhayader and Llandrindod Wells are more spectacular, forest-cloaked hills around Radnor, rising to over 2,000 ft (609 m) at Radnor Forest. Set apart from the main north-south line of the Cambrian Mountains, the scenery is never less than impressive from the hills of the forest, giving superb views across into Wales and east into England.

Another lovely feature of this area is the unusually-named 'Water-break-its neck' waterfall, which plunges 70 ft (21m) into a wooded glen near New Radnor.

Yet more classic Welsh moorland scenery is to be found at Mynydd Eppynt (the 'Mountain of the Wild Ponies'). Lonely minor roads cross the moors giving easy access to a landscape that can be both exhilarating and intimidating at the same time - particularly around dusk on a cold winter's evening! As you drive, cycle or walk through this wild landscape look out for the tough little Welsh mountain ponies from which the hills derive their name.

The complete opposite of this landscape is the wooded valleys and fields of the lowland areas between the hills, which have been farmed for centuries. At spots such as Builth Wells you can relax by the River Wye on a warm summer day and feel time slip by - before you put on your boots and head up into the hills!

Elan Valley

History and Culture

Just because Mid-Wales is a little off the beaten track doesn't mean to say nothing has ever happened here! Take a look at any good map of the area and you'll see that everywhere are signs of the past - prehistoric cromlechs and tumuli on mountain tops; Roman camps on commanding promontories; and the remains of Norman and medieval castles and churches (some being rather than more remains and still in use today).

One of the best-known features from the distant past is Offa's Dyke, an ancient earthwork built by King Offa of Mercia in the 8th century as a dividing line between his kingdom and the land of the Welsh princes to the east. The dyke runs 177 miles along the border from Prestatyn to Chepstow and there are impressive remains in places such as Llanfair Hill, just north of Knighton. The Offa's Dyke Heritage Centre is also located in the town.

The border area was for centuries an area of contention between the Welsh and the English. For instance, King Harold (the same one who came to a sticky end in 1066) developed New Radnor in 1064 as a stronghold commanding a valley leading from the English border into Wales (prior to this Old Radnor had been the administrative centre for the area). After Harold's defeat at the Battle of Hastings the town was developed on a grid iron pattern by the Normans, who also built town walls and a castle, although little remains of them today.

Later the town was again in the thick of things when it fell to Cromwell's troops in 1644 during the English Civil War. Wales' last native prince knew this part of his kingdom well, and died here. Prince Llywelyn was killed in battle with the English in 1282 at the village of Cilmery, near Builth Wells (a roadside monument marks the spot), and is said to be buried at the remote but beautifully located Abbey Cwmhir. The remains of the abbey, which dates back to 1143, are just one of a number of interesting religious sites in Mid-Wales. Abbey Cwmhir was once the site of the largest church in Wales, whilst close by the tiny little church at Llananno with its magnificent rood screen is at the opposite end of the scale.

The traditional means of making a living in this part of the world has been, and still is (although for how much longer?) farming. Sheep and to a lesser extent Welsh hill ponies on the uplands, grazing and crops on the lowland. (You can see the area's rich agricultural heritage in all its glory at the annual Royal Welsh Show in Builth Wells each July - definitely not to be missed if you're in the area.)

Tourism became important for Mid-Wales' various spa towns in the 19th century - Llanwrtyd Wells, tiny Llangammarch Wells, Builth Wells and Llandrindod Wells all developed as a result of the 18th and 19th century craze for 'taking the waters'. Now, of course, people tend to take to the waters in rather more exotic climates, but these towns have been left with an interesting and attractive legacy of spa-related buildings such as pump rooms and hotels. Llandrindod Wells celebrates this past every summer with its popular Victorian Festival.

Indeed, many towns in the Heart of Wales have some fine architectural sites from the past - Rhayader, for example, with the 14th century Triangle Inn and Presteigne with some fine Georgian houses along Broad Street.

Around the same time as the spa towns hit their peak, the railways arrived in Mid-Wales, and the Heart of Wales Line and the Central Wales Line are still two of the most scenic routes in Britain - and a great way to explore the area without a car.

Those early tourists who visited the area via the railways or horse and carriage and discovered the hills, lakes, forests and valleys would still recognise most of Mid-Wales today. The beautiful landscape and scenery has changed little, the towns and villages are attractive as ever, and we have the advantage, as of course, of being able to get here much more easily than could those early travellers.

Many of the working traditions of Mid-Wales are continued today by craftspeople working throughout the area. Many will allow you to visit their workshops and see their skills first-hand - potters, weavers, jewellers and woodcarvers all use traditional skills to produce lasting souvenirs of this lovely corner of Wales.

Wildlife

For many visitors one of Mid-Wales' major attractions is the wildlife, especially the birds, and in particular the red kite. This graceful yet impressive raptor can take on all the hues of an autumn forest when the sun shines across its feathers, and it has almost become the emblem of Mid-Wales.

Most visitors who take the time to scan the skies of the quieter upland areas are likely to catch a glimpse of a red kite hanging effortlessly on a thermal, or soaring without so much as a flap of its wings across the moorland skies, and the one sure way of recognising it is by the distinctive forked tail.

Yet it's only recently that the red kite has become so numerous - although once it was so common it could be seen on the street of London. Persecution over the centuries meant that by the 1930's only two breeding pairs were left in the country, surviving in the lonely hills of Mid-Wales. In recent times a concerted effort has been made to help the kite's number increase again, and this has been so successful that by 1995 120 pairs were raising 112 young. There are still problems from unimaginative individuals who either collect the eggs or poison the birds, but now visitors are actively encouraged to visit the area specifically to view red kites through the Kite Country project. For more details of their work contact Kite Country, The Bank, Newtown, Powys SY16 2AB (01686 624143).

Of course, there's more to the Heart of Wales than just the spectacular red kite - the moorlands may also reveal golden plover, ring ouzel, the curlew with its distinctive cry resonant of Britain's high country, maybe even merlins, goshawks and peregrines. Buzzards and ravens are a common site almost everywhere. In the woodlands you can expect to hear if not see warblers, flycatchers and redstarts, and on summer nights you may also hear the strange churring call of the nightjar or grasshopper warbler, whilst in wetter areas coot, mallard, great crested grebe, kingfishers, dippers and herons can be seen.

Mammals are relatively abundant - the ubiquitous rabbit, fox, grey squirrel and badger, of course, occur almost everywhere, but if you're lucky you may get a rare view of a pine marten, polecat or even an otter. The otter is everyone's favourite, but despite his popularity he certainly doesn't perform for his potential audience. Your best bet of seeing an otter is at night, as they're mostly nocturnal creatures. Also at night, especially around dusk, keep an eye out for bats, which are quite common - and won't get caught in your hair, however close they may come! Underwater things are pretty busy too, with some excellent fishing on the Wye, especially for salmon and trout. You may also catch crayfish in some of the tributaries.

The above scarcely does justice to the wildlife of the area though. For more details call in at one of the many information centres where expert advice will help you follow up your own particular interest, whether it flies, swims or runs!

Activities

If you're into the great outdoors you've hit the right place once you arrive in Mid-Wales. With all those hills and valleys, forests, rivers and lakes to go at you're not likely to be stuck for something to do.

Walking is obviously one of the best-established activities in the area, and there are no end of footpaths and bridleways throughout Mid-Wales which will allow you to explore. One of the most popular areas for walkers is the Elan Valley (but it's still never crowded). There are gentle walking trails around the spectacular dams, or more challenging routes over the moors, whilst Mynydd Eppynt and Radnor Forest also offer exhilarating walking and great views. And, of course, once you're back down in the valleys you'll never be far from a tea-shop or pub in which to reward yourself and refuel after your exertions. The area's bridleways also provide some great pony-trekking, either across the hills or through more pastoral landscapes such as the Wye Valley. Builth Wells is a popular pony trekking centre, as is Llanwrtyd Wells.

Llanwrtyd Wells has also established itself as one of Wales' major centres for mountain biking. The trails around the local hills and forests, not to mention the spectacular Llyn Brianne dam are amongst the best in Wales, although the Elan Valley and Rhayader are equally challenging - and within easy reach of anyone on a weekend visit.

Cyclists will also enjoy the quiet lanes of Mid-Wales. No buffeting from trucks or cars spewing fumes, just the bleat of sheep in the fields and brooks running alongside the road. The Welsh National Cycle Route from Holyhead to Cardiff runs right through the area, with a choice of trails depending on your fitness, whilst many towns have developed local guided and signposted route networks - amongst these are Knighton, Presteigne and Llanwrtyd Wells.

The rivers of Mid-Wales have some excellent fishing - for instance the Irfon at Llangammarch Wells is good for trout, whilst the picturesque valley of the Wye at Aberedw is also popular. Dry and wet fly fishing is also possible on the dams of the Elan Valley. Also on the water, the canoeing can be excellent.

Victorian Festival - Llandrindod Wells

The Wye again is a popular venue at a variety of locations, although make sure you're not on the water in a fishing area!

Mid-Wales also has a number of top golf courses set amidst tremendous and secluded scenery, such as at Llandrindod Wells where you'll be teeing off 1,000 feet above sea level - what better way to enjoy a round or two on a warm summer day?

There is also a wide range of leisure centres and swimming pools at most major towns in the area, offering everything from leisure pools and flumes to climbing walls and bouncy castles. Some centres also have disabled facilities - see 'Sports and Activities in the Heart of Wales' for more details.

And finally, if you want something really different, how about bog snorkelling? This sport is exactly what is sounds, and is unique to Mid-Wales. The World Championships are held every summer at Llanwrtyd Wells, where competitors have to snorkel two length of a 60-yard course. Competitors from all over the world have been attracted to this peculiarly Welsh form of eccentricity - in fact the 1992 champion was from Australia. All you need is the right attitude, plenty of shower gel, and enough summer rain (believe it or not the event was cancelled in 1995 because of a drought - in Mid-Wales!

Getting There

Far from the crowds, but not hard to get to - you may be surprised at just how accessible Mid-Wales is. Served by the Shrewsbury - Swansea Heart of Wales line and a good network of 'A' roads, even the remotest village in Mid-Wales isn't much more than three hours from London, and less from Birmingham and Manchester.

And once you're here there's a wide range of accommodation to suit all budgets, from excellent campsites and youth hostels to B&B's and top hotels. Add great pubs and restaurants and you've got all you need.

So what are you waiting for?!

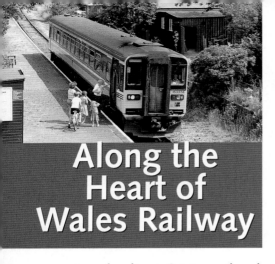

Along the Heart of Wales Railway

Few railway lines in Britain pass through such splendid scenery as the Heart of Wales railway. Hop aboard as we enjoy a brief train journey through classic Welsh countryside.

Leaving medieval Shrewsbury and the high hills of the Long Mynd, the Heart of Wales railway runs 120 miles beyond the green, rolling hills of the borderlands to the higher, tree-clad slopes of Radnor and the Brecon Beacons.

Built in sections by several companies, the line began in Llanelli sometime after 1839 and was used to transport anthracite from the Amman Valley. Soon passengers were travelling in open carriages in the summer sun and little worried at the lack of a timetable or proper stations. The next stretch to be built was to Llandeilo; Shrewsbury to Craven Arms was completed in 1851; and Llandovery station opened in 1858. The opening of each link in the chain from south to north (or north to south!) was usually accompanied by banquets, music and celebrations, and the final link, from Llandrindod to Llandovery, was completed in 1868.

The various companies that developed the line were bought out by the London North Western Railway and the Great Western Railway in 1889, and despite

Llanwrtyd Wells

Beeching's savage axing of rural lines in the 60's and recent privatisation the Heart of Wales Line is still up and running and providing a fine service for commuters, hoilday makers, day trippers and locals as well as being a valuable piece of the nation's history and heritage.

Slipping away to the west at Craven Arms, the train heads towards central Wales along a single-track lifeline. Our first stop is Knighton, the mid point of the Offa's Dyke earthworks, an 8th-century fortification 80 miles long which defines much of the border of England and Wales 1200 years after it was first erected for precisely that purpose.

As with many of the towns and villages from here on, much of Knighton's charm and interest derives from its refusal to bow to the demands of fashionable development, and it retains many of the characteristic features of a traditional market town.

As the train's single carriage rolls away from Knighton, it passes the hills, forests, rivers and ubiquitous sheep which characterise this landscape; over the thirteen arches of Knucklas viaduct; through one of the pretiest stations on the line, Dolau ('Dolly' to the locals); and on to Llandrindod Wells, the largest and most famous of Mid-Wales' Victorian spa towns. It was to the wells of Llandrindod, Builth, Llangammarch and Llanwrtyd that this railway line brought thousands of visitors from the English and Welsh conurbations during the Victorian and Edwardian eras. Here they sought cures for a variety of ailments using the magical properties of the saline, sulphurous or barium chloride waters. With this explosion in the number of visitors came a boom in building to provide for them - hotels, pavilions, shopping emporia and villas. Much of the architecture from the 1860s to the 1930s remains intact and little altered. Llandrindod, spacious and unhurried and

noted for its bowling facilities, celebrates its Victorian heyday each August.

From here the train heads for Builth on the River Wye, home of the Royal Welsh Show, the Wyeside Arts Centre and regular collector's fairs. Then on through Cilmery, where Llywelyn, the last native Prince of Wales, was killed by the English in 1282; rolling further to Llangammarch at the foot of the Eppynt hills; and next stop on the line, Llanwrtyd, one of many which claims to be the smallest town in Britain (and maybe it is).

Llanwrtyd has a red kite centre, and annual events and competitions devoted to beer drinking, a man-versus-horse race, and bog snorkelling - eccentrics will feel right at home here! Surrounded by glorious countryside, Llanwrtyd is an excellent centre for walking and mountain biking.

From Llanwrtyd our not-quite-express train rattles on to its next major link along the line, Llandovery, a bustling market town and tourist centre, described by George Borrow in 1854 as 'the pleasantest little town in which I have halted in the course of my wanderings'. Llandovery has a lively theatre and several bookshops and is a fine base

from which to explore the Tywi valley and the unique Dolaucothi gold mines.

Llandeilo, the next stop, has been dropped in a magnificent setting, and is the best centre for visiting Carreg Cennen and Dinefwr castles and the landscaped Dinefwr Park, managed by the National Trust. As we approach Llandybie and its 18-hole golf course and the delightful Glynhir waterfall nearby the end is in sight. From here the train leaves the idyllic rural landscape of Mid-Wales and travels towards the old industrial centres of South Wales. Pontarddulais has recently been attractively updated, and Llanelli, 15 minutes from Swansea, embraces a new leisure centre, a motor racing circuit and the Pembrey Country Park. And from March 2000 it will be the centre for the Millennium Coastal Park, a spectacular new development along 22 kms of coastline.

And so, almost four hours, 34 stops and 120 miles after leaving Shrewsbury, the journey along the scenic line Heart of Wales line terminates in the city of Swansea - for some the end of the line, for others simply the beginning of a great little train journey.

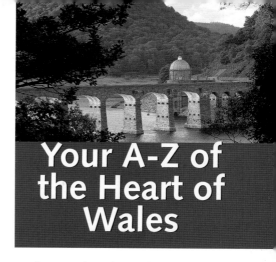

Abbey Cwmhir

This remote village lies north-east of Rhayader and north-west of Llandrindod Wells, and is surrounded by woodland and hills. One of the first things you will notice upon entering the village is the interesting inn, named the Happy Union. The church opposite, built in 1836, has an interesting Light of the World window and the stone coffin lid of Abbot Mabli, who died in 1200.

The remains of the great abbey are the showpiece of this village. They lie among a scatter of elms and sycamores below the road in a river meadow. Only parts of the walls remain, with the bases of what must have been truly magnificent columns. It is said that the body of Llywelyn, the last Prince of Wales, was buried under the high altar. The abbey was founded in 1143 by Cadwallon ap Madog, a cousin of Rhys ap Gruffydd who was the founder of Whitland Abbey. The first

Your A-Z of the Heart of Wales

monks were brought in from Whitland. Henry III plundered the abbey to avenge the misdirection of some of his soldiers by a friar, but it was Owain Glyndwr who destroyed it, believing that the monks were spies for the English. At the Dissolution there were only three monks left here. The nave was the longest in Wales.

River Wye

Aberedw

The village of Aberedw, which sits behind a massive, protective rock outcrop, is approached by twisting roads through the Wye Valley. Its square-towered church, St Cewydd, is tucked away from the road behind a row of cottages. Interesting features include an impressive porch and a 15th-century screen. A railway line, now closed, cuts through the remains of Llywelyn's Castle. Some of the stones of the castle were used as ballast when the line was built.

Builth Wells

This market town is set in a lush and beautiful section of the Wye Valley. It added Wells to its name after Lady Hester Stanhope, the niece of the younger Pitt, stayed nearby at the beginning of the 19th century. It was during the Victorian era that the town became a popular place to take the waters, first discovered during 1830. Today the waters are no longer consumed, but Builth has gained a new importance by becoming the permanent headquarters of the Royal Welsh Show. For one crowded week in summer every year it becomes the agricultural capital of Wales.

Livestock sales are also held regularly at the showground. The grounds lie across the river at Llanelwedd and are joined to the main town by a many-arched bridge. There is a pleasant tree-lined walk along the river bank. Overlooking the river on the south side is the flourishing Wyeside Arts Centre, which holds a regular programme of concerts, theatre, films and art exhibitions. The 14th-century church of St Mary's has been extensively rebuilt, and the remains of the once important castle are buried under grassy mounds behind the Lion Hotel.

Builth is a pony-trekking centre with hillsides above the Wye. To the south of Builth, the Wye runs through wooded hills

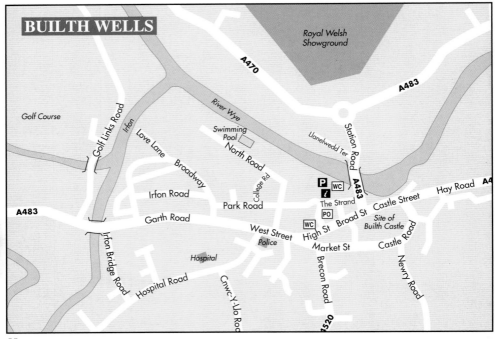

Tawny Owl Animal Park & Craft Centre

Near Hay on Wye

Animal Park

Meet Basil one of our mischievous goats and all his other funny friends!

Craft Centre

Beautiful Country Crafts from all over the UK. A must for presents.
Childrens Play Area with tractor track
Picnic area
Public toilets with disabled & baby change facilities
Entrance to Craft Centre only is Free

**Open all week except Wednesdays
10am-5.30pm April-September
10.30am-4pm October-December**
Directions: take the A438 Hereford to Brecon road into village of Clyro then follow brown tourist signs to park

The Park is family run and situated in breathtaking country side surrounded by broadleaved woodlands where Tawny Owls live.

The Craft Centre has many traditional country crafts beautifully handmade using methods passed down from generation to generation. The crafts come from all over the UK and at certain times of the year, visitors may enjoy demonstrations by crafts people who take pride in their work and keep the rural crafts alive.

We have farm tours by arrangement with lots of hands-on experience. There are several walks to enjoy with wellie boot hire. We cater for birthday parties for children up to age 8 and provide tea with lots of fun and games.

We also have accommodation to let in our holiday cottage which sleeps 4.

Put aside a couple of hours and come and experience something for the whole family.

Wern Newydd, Painscastle, Builth Wells, Powys LD2 3JW
TELEPHONE 01497 851 399

which become dramatically rocky at Aberedw. It is popular with fishermen, and downstream it also attracts enthusiastic white-water canoeists. At Erwood, in a particularly fine section of the stream, a light bridge crosses the Wye. In the old days this was the place where the drovers urged their cattle through the shallows on their way to the markets of England. There are some beautiful walks on Mynydd Epynt, east of the B4519.

Wyeside Arts Centre The Centre is housed in a fascinating Victorian Market Hall building on the famous Wye bridge in the centre of Builth Wells. Sympathetically converted to provide two auditoria, a gallery, foyer and bars, Wyeside has a full year-round programme of arts & entertainment, films, exhibitions and workshops.

Wyeside's Live Show programme covers a wide variety of events, ranging from theatre, opera, and music from classical orchestras to comedy, ballet and modern dance and events for children. The emphasis is always on quality and value for money. The gallery offers a wide range of exhibitions including, paintings, sculpture and photography, and the beautifully designed foyer craft cases feature a wide variety of craft-work, such as ceramics, wood, jewellery, glass, silk, leather, slate, and much more.

The cinema, recently expensively re-equipped to provide Dolby stereo sound and a bigger, brighter screen, offers the chance to see the best current releases as well as regular foreign/art house films.

Wyeside Arts Centre has recently been substantially remodelled with European funding, and its new foyer/coffee bar provides an attractive welcome to the Centre. The all-floor lift gives wheelchair access to the full range of the Centre's facilities, and infra-red sound enhancement systems are now installed in both cinema and live show auditoria. Hence Wyeside is well established as one of Wales' busiest and most exciting small arts centres.

The Royal Welsh The development of the Royal Welsh showground has been a continuing process since the show moved permanently to Llanelwedd, Builth Wells, 36 years ago. More than 1000 tradestands and shops bring the buzz of business to the showground. The Royal Welsh is designed to cater for all tastes, young and old. The show celebrates its centenary in 2001.

Cilmery

The village of Cilmery, a few miles west of Builth Wells, recalls the moment in Welsh history that effectively prevented any possible hope of uniting Wales against Edward I. According to tradition it was here that Llywelyn, the last native Prince of Wales, was killed by an English soldier in 1282 after failing to gain support from the townspeople and garrison at Builth. At the roadside near the spot where Llywelyn is said to have died is a plaque and a huge granite memorial stone. Llywelyn's Cave, where the prince went into hiding to escape the English forces, is at Aberedw. Visitors to the village can enjoy all the hospitality of the 14th-century Prince Llewelyn Inn, where there is ample parking and the attractions include good food, a beer garden and a children's play area.

Clyro

This peaceful village, situated off the A413, is just across the river from Hay-on-Wye. Some of the original 13th-century church survives, although it was rebuilt by J Nicholson in 1853. The Rev Francis Kilvert was curate here from 1865-1872, and his famous diary – selected and edited by William Plomer – opens with the last two of these years. The diary gives a charming picture of the Radnorshire people and countryside of Kilvert's day. A tablet to his

ERWOOD STATION CRAFT CENTRE

Alan & Erika Cunningham. Tel: 01982 560674

★ A friendly and engaging craft centre in the heart of Wales; once a G.W.R. station, now supporting local craftspeople and artists.

★ Resident woodturner, Alan Cunningham – National Eisteddfod prize-winner.
Commissions ~ Demonstrations ~ Courses.

★ An attractive location by the river Wye. Ample parking/picnic site and superb walks.

★ Excellent coffee and cakes.

★ Open every day, March – December.

★ Directions: 6 miles South of Builth Wells on B4567. Follow tourist signs from A470.

Erwood Station Crafts Centre This friendly and engaging centre displays the work of over 50 local craftspeople and artists, and it is housed in the former station of the Great Western Railway which was closed in 1962. Resident woodturner Alan Cunningham, a twice National Eisteddfod prize-winner, can be seen in his workshop creating all types of crafted work from local timber. Alan Cunningham also offers demonstrations and courses. Erwood Station Crafts is open 7 days a week from mid-February to end of December, 9.00am to 6.00pm in the spring and summer, and 10.00am to 5.00pm in the autumn and winter. The Centre is 6 miles south of Builth Wells, on the B4567, and is well signposted from the A470. For more information ring 01982 560674.

Kerry

This quiet village, situated on the edge of the Kerry Forest, is about three miles east of Newtown. It has an ancient church with powerful Romanesque arcading. It is unique among the small churches of Wales for there is a complete description of its consecration in 1170. Kerry is one of the few villages in Wales that has given its name to a breed of sheep. This large, sturdy, animal originated on the steep, close-cropped Kerry Hills to the south of the village. This is great grazing country, and great walking country as well. An ancient trackway runs the whole length of the hills, lifted high above the tumbled landscape, with fine views to the north.

Knighton

This little grey-stone town with a clock tower at its heart gives the impression that it is clinging desperately to the sides of the steep hill on which it has grown. The Saxons settled here first, then the Welsh arrived in 1052, to be quickly followed by the Normans soon after 1066. The Normans built the first castle – a timber structure on a mound

memory can be found on Ashbrook House, where he lived.

A detour from the village takes you to Maesyronnel Chapel, which is set on a steep hillside, half a mile off the A438 near Glasbury (see Hay-on-Wye on page xx).

Elan Valley See Page 112.

Erwood

Seven miles south of Builth Wells, on one of the most attractive stretches of the River Wye, this pretty little village was originally called Y Rhyd, meaning 'The Ford'. Erwood is associated with Llywelyn the Last Prince, and the men of Edward I probably crossed the river here when they were hunting him. These days a bridge spans the river. It is believed that the concept of Punch magazine was conceived here when Henry Mayhew stayed at the local inn. Llangoed Castle lies two miles south-east and was rebuilt in 1911, though a south porch – dating from 1632 has been preserved.

situated behind the Smithfield and still called Bryn-y-Castell. The first stone castle was built on the other side of the town on the top of a hill in the 12th century, and the mound and remnants of a ditch are still visible.

Knighton's situation in the Teme Valley on the Welsh/English border, with the river's heavily wooded and mountainous left bank nearby, is delightful. The Welsh name for Knighton is 'Tref-y-Clawdd', meaning the Town on the Dyke, and Offa's Dyke runs all along the west side. This is a good starting point for walks along the 8th-century barrier put up by King Offa of Mercia as a dividing line between his kingdom and Welsh territory.

Offa's earthen wall and ditch ran for much of the length of Wales, from Chepstow to Prestatyn. As well as being a political barrier, the dyke served as a kind of customs point, controlling the movement of cattle and trade.

Remnants of this ancient earthwork can still be seen in many locations along the border. One of its best-preserved sections is at Llanfair Hill, about five miles north of Knighton, where the top of the ditch to the bottom of the ditch measures 16 ft. The Offa's Dyke Heritage Centre is housed in a new, purpose-built centre on West Street, where you can find information on short local walks and an exhibition on the dyke's history. Call 01457 529424 for more details. In the Riverside Park, behind the centre, a stone monument marks the opening of the 177-mile-long Offa's Dyke National Trail in 1971.

The Central Wales railway line runs through Knighton. The station is a little gem of Victorian-gothic railway architecture. This is because Sir Richard Green-Price, who released the land for the track, did so only on condition that he should personally approve

PUBLIC TRANSPORT IN POWYS

The County of Powys extends to a quarter of Wales, from the Snowdonia National Park down to the South Wales Valleys, and offers a huge variety of places to visit by public transport. Local buses run through the unspoiled countryside and through many bustling market towns. Royal Mail Postbus services can take you deep into the countryside and through some of the most awe inspiring scenery in Wales. The scenic railways include the Heart of Wales Line that is 120 miles long and runs from Shrewsbury to Swansea, and the Shrewsbury to Aberystwyth Line that connects with the Cambrian Coast Line. These two railways are amongst the most beautiful in Britain. The County also has two of the "Great Little Trains of Wales", the Welshpool and Llanfair Light Railway and the Brecon Mountain Railway.

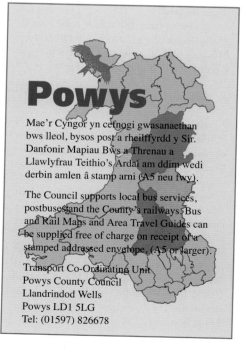

Mae'r Cyngor yn cefnogi gwasanaethan bws lleol, bysos post a rheilffyrdd y Sir. Danfonir Mapiau Bws a Threnau a Llawlyfrau Teithio's Ardal am ddim wedi derbin amlen â stamp arni (A5 neu fwy).

The Council supports local bus services, postbuses and the County's railways. Bus and Rail Maps and Area Travel Guides can be supplied free of charge on receipt of a stamped addressed envelope, (A5 or larger).

Transport Co-Ordinating Unit
Powys County Council
Llandrindod Wells
Powys LD1 5LG
Tel: (01597) 826678

Knighton

the design of all stations, bridges, and other structures to be built in the area. The town contains a number of interesting old inns. The double-naved church, originally Norman, has been twice rebuilt. It is one of the few Welsh churches dedicated to an English saint, and the only one to St Edward.

The most picturesque street in Knighton is The Narrows, which runs uphill from the Clock Tower. Right opposite the tower is the town's prettiest house – a narrow-fronted half-timbered building set back behind a delightfully paved courtyard. Every May the town holds a fair and an Agricultural Show and Carnival. Ruins of a Roman villa were discovered two miles outside the town in the hamlet of Stow during 1925.

Offa's Dyke Heritage Centre Situated in West Street, the Centre is open all year round and has a permanent exhibition for walkers and other visitors. For further information ring 01547 528192.

Powys Observatory For further information ring 01547 520247.

Llanbister

The size of the fortress-like church at Llanbister, just north of Llandrindod Wells, is an indication of the ancient village's importance as the centre of the old kingdom of Rhwng Gwy a Hafren (between Wye and Severn). This modest kingdom was further reduced by the old Welsh law which required that the overlord's property be inherited equally by each of his sons. The result was the creation of smaller lordships, one of which was Maelienydd, centred on Llanbister. The name is now given to an area of open hill land to the east of the village. One of the village's landmarks is the Lion Hotel, on whose sign is a golden lion – reputedly the crest of an 11th-century king. The same heraldic lion also formed part of the coat of arms adopted by the former Radnorshire County Council.

Llandinam

On more than one occasion, Llandinam has been awarded the title of 'Best Kept Village in Wales'. Colourful gardens line the A470 alongside the river Severn, and the black-and-white timbered houses of the village centre are set well back from the main road. The beautifully maintained little church overlooks the village, which is certainly worth a detour.

Llandrindod Wells

After the grey stone and slate so characteristic of Welsh towns and villages, Llandrindod Wells comes as a surprise with its towers, turrets, cupolas, balconies, oriels, colonnades, ornamental ironwork, loggias and balustrades. The town has magnificent gardens, parks, green banks and commons.

The town grew up around healing springs that rise here. Llandrindod emerged as a spa around 1670, but it did not reach its heyday until the second half of the 19th century. After a slow influx of visitors from the beginning of the century, William Grosvenor of Shrewsbury came to test the waters for himself. He was impressed and decided that the spa had a future, in which case hotel accommodation would become a necessity. He took a lease on the farm beside the little church up on the hill and converted it into the Grand Hotel.

After 1815 and the end of the Anglo-French wars, people began to visit Llandrindod in greater numbers, mostly staying at the Pump Room. The coming of the railway in 1866 took Llandrindod into its golden years. With the passing of a local enclosure act, building land became available, and the streets that now form the town centre were constructed. In 1871 a new church was built and at first called Christ Church, but later renamed Holy Trinity to avoid confusion with the Congregational Christ Church. In 1895 the

Victorian Festival - Llandrindod Wells

old church up on the hill was restored and re-opened, and when the Church in Wales became disestablished from the Church of England it was here that the first Archbishop of Wales was elected.

Llandrindod Wells became the ecclesiastical capital of Wales, with the governing body of the Church in Wales holding its meetings here and other departments also finding the town a convenient half-way point between north and south for committee meetings. When Llandrindod Wells was at the height of its popularity as a spa, 80,000 visitors would come to it in a season, with peers, judges, ambassadors, and other celebrities among them. Spa treatment went out of fashion, however, and Llandrindod declined. In the 1960s the Pump Room closed, in recent years the old Pump House has been refurbished.

An annual drama festival is held in the grandly-named Albert Hall at the beginning

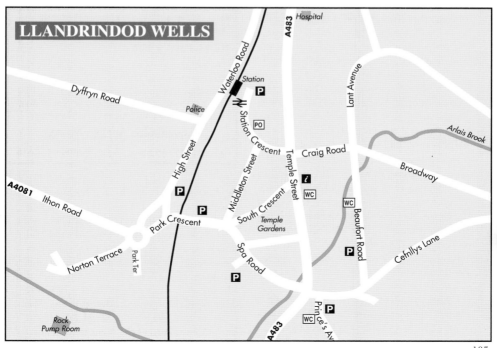

of May, and the atmosphere of yesteryear is re-created in the town every August for the week-long Victorian Festival, when everyone from the butcher to the baker dons the traditional costume of the period.

It is also a good touring centre for the attractive countryside around. The important Roman camp at Castell Collen, near Llanyre on the west bank of the Ithon, has been excavated and the lover of old and unusual churches will find some unexpected delights. For example, south of Llandrindod, the church at Disserth still retains its old box pews and on the road that leads north from Llandrindod to the Kerry Hills and Newtown, the church at Llanbister still has its 18th-century singing loft, where psalms were led by the village band. At the little church of Llananno, rebuilt in the 19th century, is a magnificent carved rood screen – a medieval masterpiece.

Little wonder that Llandrindod Wells is such a popular centre for holidaymakers wanting to discover the very heart of Wales.

Llandrindod Wells & Radnorshire Museum Situated in the centre of Llandrindod Wells, the museum houses exhibits relating to the history of the old Mid Wales county of Radnorshire. Displays illustrate the largely rural farming lifestyle of the area as well as the development of Llandrindod Wells as a country spa resort during the Victorian and Edwardian era. The museum also displays material relating to fine art, costume and the prehistoric, Roman and medieval history of the area, including the Roman fort of Castell Collen.

The Red Kite Centre opened in 1995. Set on the museum's first floor, this exhibition highlights the lifestyle and successful fight back from the edge of extinction by Britain's most beautiful bird of prey. The exhibition also includes a video and computer information station. For further information ring 01597 824513.

Rock Park Spa You can experience a wide range of complimentary treatments at the Rock Spa Health Centre, as well as sampling the saline waters that Llandrindod was once so famous for. There is also an interesting new exhibition at the centre - for more information ring 01597 822997.

National Cycle Exhibition. An imaginative exhibition set in the heart of wonderful cycling and mountain biking country. Exhibits range from over 120 cycles of all ages to tributes to great British cyclists such as Tom Simpson, 1965 world professional road race champion. The exhibition is based in the Automobile Palace - for more details call 01597 825531.

Llangammarch Wells

Situated at the confluence of the Cammarch and Irfon rivers, Llangammarch Wells stands on the scenic Heart of Wales railway line. Its waters – once prescribed for certain heart conditions – were considered to be of the highest quality in Britain. The Pump Room still exists in the grounds of the Lake Hotel.

Today's visitors come to the village for the fishing (the Irfon is a good trout river) and the tranquillity of the surroundings. Llangammarch stands at the northern end of Mynydd Epynt – a large, empty area of high moorland, where a road climbs up a steep-sided valley from the town. From the summit, there are glorious views northwards and eastwards across the mountains and borderlands of Mid Wales.

Llanwrtyd Wells

This little town dates from 1732, when Theophilus Evans – the grandfather of the historian Theophilus Jones – saw a frog disporting itself in the sulphurous waters. Since these waters apparently did not harm the frog, he thought that they might be worth trying as a cure for scurvy, from which he suffered. He began drinking them, found his condition improved, and came to the conclusion that these were healing waters. So Llanwrtyd became a spa, and the wells at Dol-y-Coed still exist. Nowadays the little town is no longer visited by those in search of health, but by holidaymakers who come for the scenery and pony trekking – which is one of the specialities of the area.

On the outskirts of the town towards Builth Wells, on the A483, is Cambrian Woollen Mill. Founded in 1820 and now in private ownership, it is one of the few remaining woollen mills in Wales. Production focuses on woollen goods and crafts, and you can enjoy a fascinating tour of the mill to see how wool is carded, spun and woven. The mill shop also gives you an opportunity to take home a special gift or memento of your visit. The mill is open from Monday to Friday (9.30am to 5.00pm) throughout the year, and also on Saturday between Easter and the end of October. For more information ring 01591 610211.

The picturesque spa town of Llanwrtyd Wells has several fine hotels which provide an ideal base for walking, pony trekking, horse riding, fishing, mountain biking, touring and a hundred and one other activities. The town's Tourist Information Centre is open six days a week from Easter to mid-October, and on Thursday-Saturday inclusive between mid-October and Easter. It houses the Red Kite Centre, which shows remarkable live pictures of a goshawk's nest and a blue tit's box, along with recorded pictures of barn owls and red kites, from April to August.

World Bog Snorkelling Championships
Eccentricity is certainly not a trait exclusive to the English - as this madcap annual

charity competition in Llanwrtyd Wells proves! A channel, 60 yards long, has been cut through a peat bog on the outskirts of the town and competitors have to swim two lengths, wearing a snorkel. The winner is the person who completes the course in the fastest time, with modest cash prizes awarded in three categories - world champion, female world champion and local champion. Past winners include an Australian from Perth in 1992, and in the scorching summer of 1995 no competition could be held because of the drought! The World Bog Snorkelling Championships - surely one to look out for in future Olympics - are organised by Gordon Green of the town's Neuadd Arms Hotel. For more information ring 01591 610236.

Red Kite Mountain Bike Centre & ***Welsh Wayfaring Holidays*** Based at Neuadd Arms Hotel, Llanwrtyd Wells. For more information see page 125, or ring 01591 610236.

Bog Snorkelling

River Irfon, Nr Llanwrtyd Wells

*1999/2000 Festivals & Events,
Llanwrtyd Wells* A full programme detailing
these interesting and varied events is
available from the town's Tourist Information
Centre. Ring or fax 01591 610666.

New Radnor

New Radnor was founded by King
Harold to replace Old Radnor as the
administrative centre of the district. Walls
and a castle protected it, and traces of the
walls can be seen in a field at the end of a
rough lane running off the Rhayader road on
the left, just beyond the church. The castle
stood behind the church, but nothing is left
of it now except the mound. With the high
summits of Radnor Forest behind and the
Smatcher in front, both closing in on each
other to the south-west, the town was only
vulnerable from the east.

Water Street actually has a stream
running down it, and small bridges to allow
access to the houses. At its lower end is a
monument somewhat resembling the Albert
Memorial in London. This is a memorial to
Sir George Cornwall Lewis, who died in
1863. He was a baronet and MP for the
borough from 1855 until his death, and it is
thought that he might have become prime
minister if he had not died when he did. The
village is now bypassed by the A44, which
makes it a very peaceful place.

Old Radnor

This village comprises a church, school,
inn, a tiny group of council houses and a
scatter of cottages. In pre-conquest times
Old Radnor was a seat of local government
and remained so until 1064. The church,
which stands some 840 ft above sea level,
has a battlemented tower and organ casing
dating back to 1500, believed to be the oldest
in Britain. The same is believed of the font, a
massive circular block of stone with its top

surface hollowed out to form a shallow bowl. The church also includes a wonderful medieval rood screen.

Painscastle

Painscastle is a compact village which took its name from Henry I's courtier, Pain Fitz John, who either built the castle or rebuilt in stone an earlier motte-and-bailey fortress.

Just one and a half miles west of Painscastle is the hamlet of Llanbedr, famous for its association with the Rev John Price, who was vicar here in Kilvert's time. Instead of living in his vicarage he preferred a shack of dry walling roofed with thin thatch!

Presteigne

This little town is situated on the west bank of the River Lugg. Presteigne is a border town, which takes its atmosphere and its architecture from the English county of Hereford and Worcester just across the river. Like so many of these small border towns, Presteigne grew up around a Norman castle. The castle has disappeared, but its site is now a public park known as The Warden. Broad Street has its Georgian houses, but the building which catches the eye is the half-timbered Radnorshire Arms Hotel. It was built as a private house in 1606, became a coaching inn in 1792, and contains a priest's chamber, a Tudor doorway and secret passages. Also of interest is the Judge's Lodging. Once described as 'Öthe most commodious and elegant apartments for a judge in all of England and Wales', this superbly refurbished Victorian building also houses the Tourist Information Centre and an exhibition on the histroy of the Radnor Borders region. Presteigne was once the county town of Radnorshire until the reconstruction of the counties in 1972.

Radnor Forest See page 112.

Rhayader

Rhayader is a busy little crossroads town in the heart of the Welsh hills. The A470 north-south road meets the east-west A44 at Rhayader's neat little clock tower. The town is one of the leading livestock markets in Mid Wales. It has four main streets named after the chief points of the compass and still retains its atmosphere of the 19th century. Its inns are even older, the oldest of them all being the Triangle, sited across the river in the district of Cwmdeuddwr, and is a partly weather-boarded building which dates from the 14th century. Nearly as old is the Cwmdeuddwr Arms on the Rhayader side of the bridge, which is of similar appearance.

Rhayader once had a castle. All that is left of it now is a large mound and a few stones in the angle between Church Street and West Street, high above the river. Upstream behind the castle is Waun Capel Park, from which a bridge leads over to a delightful sylvan riverside walk on the west bank. Extending from here to Llangurig is one of the prettiest reaches of the Wye, an eight-mile stretch of river with massive steep-sided mountains accompanying it on both banks. The scenery is really spectacular where the Marteg joins the Wye two and a half miles above Rhayader. The town was one of the centres of the Rebecca Riots last century, when men dressed as women and calling themselves Rebecca's Daughters smashed the turnpike gates as a protest against the heavy tolls. Today it is predominantly a tourist centre for the Elan Valley, which starts only three miles away. Rhayader is the first town of the Wye, so good fishing is guaranteed. The town has a small museum reflecting the bygone days of the region.

Cwmdeuddwr, although actually part of Rhayader, keeps its own identity and has its own church.

THE ELAN VALLEY

One of the few remaining areas of Wales that is truly wild. Dŵr Cymru Welsh Water's Elan Estate comprises some 70 square miles of hills and lakes and magnificent scenery.

The Elan Valley Visitor Centre (pictured above) extended and refurbished during 1997, open Easter – End of October. Audio-visual Theatre, Exhibitions, Information Centre, Café, shop and childrens play area.

Talks, Guided Walks, Birdwatching Safaris, Educational visits and many other events led by the Countryside Rangers.

Nature Trails, Self-guided Walks, Fly Fishing.

FOR FURTHER INFORMATION TELEPHONE (01597) 810898/810880

The Elan Valley and Visitor Centre

The Elan Valley comprises some 70 square miles of rugged Cambrian Mountain country with some of the most spectacular scenery in Britain. The whole area was bought by the Birmingham Corporation in 1892 to provide water for the City of Birmingham. In the 11 years that followed the Corporation built a series of dams which, rather than detracting from the wildness of the Valley seem to add to it. Now the land has been returned to the Welsh and is owned by Dŵr Cymru Welsh Water. The water supply and the catchment has been carefully protected for over a hundred years resulting in a haven for wildlife including the rare and beautiful red kite. Dŵr Cymru Welsh Water employ a team of Countryside Rangers to look after the wildlife of the area, they are based at the Elan Valley Visitor Centre and are more than pleased to help with any enquiries about the wildlife.

The Elan Valley has a wide range of attractions for the visitor whatever their reason for coming. No visit to the Valley is complete without a look around the Elan Valley Visitor Centre which is open every day from mid March to the end of October from 10am to 6pm. There are exhibitions and an audio-visual programme about the history of the Dams and the Red Kite, an Information Desk, a gift shop and café. Entry is free but voluntary contributions towards the upkeep of the Centre are gratefully received! There is an extensive picnic area at the Visitor Centre overlooking the River Elan and many more picnic tables around and about the Valley. Water sports are not permitted due to the deep, cold water and the fact that most people come to the Valley to enjoy the peace and quiet. However, the reservoirs are stocked with brown trout for dry and wet fly fishing and permits are available from R.M. Powell's newsagents (Tel: 01597 810451) or the Visitor Centre (Tel: 01597 810898).

Many come to the area to take advantage of the finest walking country in Wales and there is free and open access to the whole 70 square miles (except for on the enclosed land). There is an extensive network of waymarked footpaths and bridleways as well as several leafleted walks for people of all abilities including the Cnwch Wood Nature Trail. Between the months of May and September the Countryside Rangers run an extensive programme of events covering everything from birdwatching to local history. Unfortunately the nature of the terrain in the Valley makes many areas inaccessible to wheelchairs and pushchairs. However, the Visitor Centre and surrounding picnic area is fully accessible and the staff at the Information desk can suggest other areas to go to. The roadways through the Valley are excellent and there are many parking places with fine views across the reservoirs and hills.

Elan Valley

This extensive series of man-made lakes in the heart of the moorlands west of Rhayader has become the major tourist attraction of Mid Wales. These reservoirs were built to supply Birmingham, 73 miles away, with water, but the city fathers were not afraid to spend extra money in making their dams, all of which are faced with fine stonework and are things of architectural beauty. The middle dam at Caban Coch is especially notable and is a magnificent sight when the waters overflow in winter. After the Second World War, the system was further extended by the construction of the vast Claerwen Dam, in a side valley of the Elan – a civil engineer's dream but a conservationist's nightmare.

The history of the present dams is vividly re-told at the Visitor Centre which, located beneath the Caban Coch dam and close to the delightful 'model' village of Elan, was built in 1906-9 to house waterworks staff. The lakes form the basis of a 45,000-acre estate – an area renowned not only for the natural beauty of its open mountains, moors and oakwoods, but also for its prolific birdlife. The centre offers visitors a programme of guided walks and talks. Outside, overlooking the River Elan, is a statue of the poet Shelley (1792-1822), who lived with his first wife in a house now submerged beneath the waters of Caban Coch. When the reservoirs were constructed, eighteen farmhouses, a school and a church were destroyed. The Elan Valley Visitor Centre is in Elan Village. For further information ring 01597 810880/810898.

Gigrin Farm Trail For more information ring 01597 810243.

Marston Pottery For more information ring 01597 810875.

Rhayader Museum To find out more contact the local Tourist Information Centre.

Radnor Forest

Radnor Forest is not a true forest but an area of mountain split by numerous streams into a small, compact area of high, rounded hills. Although surrounded by hills of varying height, the Radnor Forest stands out as a distinct region on its own. A roughly triangular area about six miles in each direction, it is enclosed by main roads on all sides, giving the traveller fine views of almost every stream and hillside. Across its north side runs the main road from Knighton to Llandrindod Wells; to the south-west is the Kington to Rhayader A44 road; and to the south-east is part of the A44 to New Radnor.

Crags of Harley Dingle, views from Great Rhos or Black Mixen, Shepherd's Well, Rhiw Pool, and the spectacular Waterfall of 'Water-break-its-neck' are all of interest. The best natural waterfall in the region, 'Water-break-its-neck' tumbles 70 ft into a dark wooded glen. It lies in the Warren Plantation on the west side of Ffron Hill, and can be easily reached by footpaths to the right of the A44 about one and a half miles west of New Radnor.

The Welsh Masters of Fire and Glass

Welsh Royal Crystal is Wales' only manufacturer of hand crafted crystal ware - stem ware, tableware, gift ware, corporate gifts, presentation trophies and commission pieces. All production is carried out at our premises in Rhayader.

Each piece of Welsh Royal Crystal is handcrafted from molten glass, mouth blown and hand cut, each with their own unique feature - like a thumb print.

Welsh Royal Crystal patterns combine both traditional diamond and floral (intaglio) cutting. A unique range of Celtic themes reflecting the Welsh Celtic heritage has developed due to public interest. New items for 1999 include the miniature and millennium collection.

The design and supply of presentation trophies, corporate gifts and commission pieces is an expanding area of the company's business. Our in-house design team have created impressive unique pieces for events such as Cardiff Singer of the World; Young Welsh Singer Competition; Charter Mark (commissioned by the Cabinet Office); Achievement Wales Business Awards; Welsh Woman of the Year; Moon and Stars. As well as supplying a vast number of retail outlets we also offer a mail order service world wide.

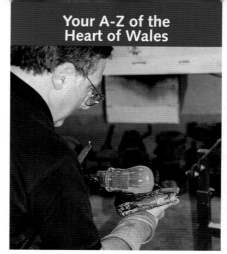

Welsh Royal Crystal

Welsh Royal Crystal Visitor Centre

Why not take a factory tour and visit the Welsh Master of Fire and Glass and wonder at the skill and craftsmanship needed to create these unique gifts? The factory shop offers a wide range of quality crystal ware and gifts at affordable prices. There is also an engraving service to personalise that special gift.

Refreshments are available in the spacious coffee shop. Disabled facilities are also provided. Sign-posted from the town clock in Rhayader, just off the A44. For further information please call, 01597 811005, fax 01597 811129, e mail Tours@welshcrystal.demon.co.uk

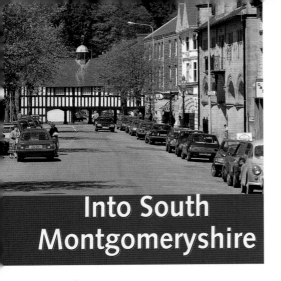

Into South Montgomeryshire

Caersws

The main railway line to Shrewsbury and London from the Cambrian coast runs through this village, as does the main road from South to North Wales. Nearly 2,000 years ago the Romans had already recognised its strategic position at the confluence of the Severn, Garno and Trannon rivers, and the outlines of the fort they built here can be traced near the railway station.

Caersws lies in the heart of typical Mid Wales country – rich meadows of the Severn backed by high hills not far from Newtown. The popular 19th century Welsh poet Ceiriog (John Hughes) was general manager of the little Van railway which ran from the main line at Caersws up to the rich Van lead mines.

At Caersws the railway leaves the Severn and follows the Carno valley westwards. Carno itself is a small village with three claims to fame. The first is in the inn with the extraordinary sign of the Aleppo Merchant. Some say it celebrates a local man who made a fortune out of Middle East trade. Others, less romantically, claim that the inn derived its name from the special pudding made here with liberal allowances of Middle East raisins. The second claim to fame is that Laura Ashley set up her first

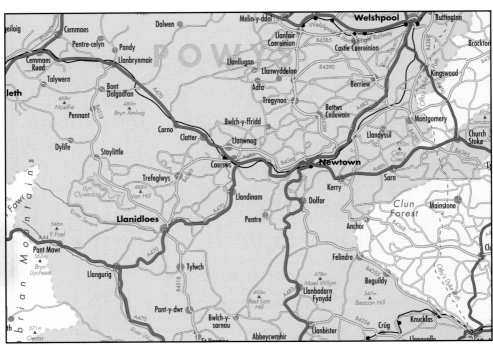

factory here in the village. And the third? You discover that just before you cross the bridge over the Severn and pass Maesmawr Hall – a fine example of oak-framed Jacobean black-and-white architecture. It is now a hotel. Many black-and-white timbered buildings, most of them farms, can be seen nearby in the upper Severn Valley.

Dylife

Dylife, high up on the eastern flank of the Plynlimon wilderness, is reached by the mountain road that winds up from Llanidloes, past Llyn Clywedog (a six-mile-long reservoir) and Staylittle. When you arrive here, you find no village – just an inn, some scattered houses and the remains of what was once one of the richest lead mines in Wales.

The Dylife stream drops into a spectacular gorge in one of the highest waterfalls in Wales – the Ffrwd Fawr. North of the mine area, a road leads off past the lonely lakes of Glaslyn and Bugeilyn into the heart of Plynlimon. On this road you will cross one of Wales' most memorable mountain roads, which climbs to a high point to offer a stunning panorama of mountain peaks. A short distance from the summit, in the direction of Machynlleth, look out for a viewpoint carved in dark slate. The late writer and broadcaster Wynford Vaughan-Thomas has been honoured by a memorial, unveiled in 1990, which must be the finest roadside viewpoint in Wales. At the road's high point, you can follow a rough track for a mile or so to the remote mountain lake of Glaslyn. There is a circular walk around the lake, which is part of the Glaslyn Nature Reserve.

Llanidloes

This attractive market town in Mid Wales is located at the junction of the Severn and Clywedog rivers, and in recent years has developed as a tourist centre. The town has a mixture of architectural styles, including Elizabethan, Georgian and Victorian. It owed its early prosperity to the lead mining in the surrounding hills and to the woollen trade. In the heart of the town stands the late 16th century timbered Market Hall. It has an open space beneath for the stalls, and a museum of local history is housed in the upper part. Such halls were common in the wool towns of Mid Wales, but this is the only surviving example. A tablet records the visit of John Wesley, who preached in the open air here at the hall. The 13th-century church is impressive and the nave contains the graceful arches which were brought here from Abbeycwmhir, after the monastery there was dissolved in 1536.

The town boasts other half-timbered houses, and there are some interesting shop fronts. Royal Arms are displayed on the fascia of Hamer's butcher's shop in Long Bridge Street. The firm held the royal warrant for three successive reigns, and served eight royal families. A life-sized red lion lives above the door of an inn of that name, and outside Higgs' shop in Great Oak Street hangs a golden lamb to indicate the sale of woollen goods.

The Town Hall in Great Oak Street was a gift from the Davies family of Llandinam in 1908, while the Trewythen Hotel opposite has associations with the Chartist riots. Rioters took three policemen prisoner and held them captive there despite the efforts of fifty other constables to rescue them. They also took a former mayor prisoner and ransacked the hotel.

The town once had a castle, but only the site – where the Mount Inn now stands – remains. The wide main street leads down from the market hall to the bridge over the Severn. The left-handed road, immediately across the bridge, leads you into the hills to the north of the Clywedog. The Llyn Clywedog Scenic Trail is two and a half miles long and starts above the car park on the

Staylittle road. It is possible to make a circuit of the lake. The route takes you through the vast Hafren Forest, which spreads over from the Clywedog valley into that of the infant Severn. The forest stretches far up the eastern slopes of Plynlimon, and the Forestry Commission has designated some attractive trails, including the Source of the Severn Walk, the Cascades Forest Trail and the Blaenhafren Falls Walk. The circuit of the lake eventually brings the motorist back into the Clywedog valley and to the area around the dam itself. Good fishing, enjoyed by a former US President during his holiday in the region, is available in the lake, under the auspices of the local angling club.

The small Bryn Tail Lead Mine site near the dam has been cleared for a well-signed industrial archaeology trail. To the east of Bryn Tail are the remains of the Van Lead Mine – once the most profitable in the region. Glyndwr's Way, part of a 121-mile walk across Powys from Knighton to Machynlleth, also crosses here.

Llanidloes Museum Situated on the ground floor of the Town Hall, Great Oak Street, the museum houses exhibits relating to the long history of this ancient market town, with its timber-framed black and white Old Market Hall. Artefacts of particular interest relate to the history of mining in the area and to the Chartist revolt of 1839. For further information contact the local Tourist Information Centre (01686 412605).

Montgomery

Montgomery is situated within a mile of the Shropshire border. It has a small square with an 18th-century town hall, Georgian houses of red brick, old inns, and half-timbered Elizabethan and Jacobean houses.

Behind the square rises the castle hill, on which Roger de Montgomery built his first stronghold in the 13th century, and from which he launched his attack on the lands of

Machynlleth

the Welsh to the west. The position of Montgomery, on a high ridge ending with a crag to the north, made it a key point in the politics of the border.

Montgomery Church is mainly 15th century, with a splendid rood screen and richly carved tombs of the Herbert family. In the graveyard is the Robber's Grave – John Davies was convicted of murder in 1821 and was buried in this corner. He swore that he was innocent, and declared that, in proof of it, nothing would grow on his grave for over a hundred years.

Beyond the church there are traces of the old walls, with a view out towards England and the east. Offa's Dyke ran close to the town, and its course can be traced from Montgomery to the Long Mountain behind Welshpool. Remains of the Dyke are preserved in Lymore Park, east of the town.

Montgomery Castle For more details

contact the local Tourist Information Centre.

Old Bell Museum For more details contact the local Tourist Information Centre.

Machynlleth

Machynlleth boasts an enchanting position in the Dovey Valley, which is a beautiful natural feature of Mid Wales. The site has been inhabited since the early Iron Age. Owain Glyndwr made it the capital of Wales, and he was proclaimed king here at a parliament in 1404; the present Institute is traditionally his Parliament House. Because of Machynlleth's position at the junction of several old coach roads, and as a great sheep-trading centre, the town had twenty-four inns in the 19th century. Four inns, the haunt of anglers fishing the Dovey, still cluster round the clock tower which marks the centre of the town. There are 17th, 18th and 19th-century houses in the street called

Maen Gwyn, and near the clock tower is Royal House, where the future Henry VII is said to have stopped in 1485.

Dyfi Centre Part of the Tourist Information Centre. Tel: 01654 702401.

King Arthur's Labyrinth at Corris Craft Centre. In the darkest of the Dark Ages, the legions of the once-mighty Roman Empire had withdrawn from Britain, leaving the native Celtic peoples to defend themselves against the increasingly powerful Saxon invaders. Out of the darkness came Arthur – destined to overcome all enemies from without and within and to bring peace to these islands. His feats of bravery, supernatural powers and strength of leadership spelled defeat for the forces of darkness and, in a time when history was recorded only by word of mouth and passed on by bards and storytellers, tales of Arthur's

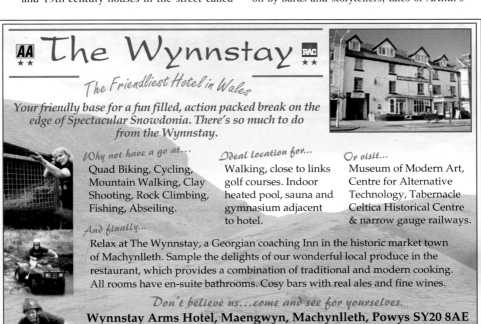

great deeds spread throughout the land, gradually transcending the boundary between fact and legend as they as they were handed on from one generation to the next.

King Arthur's Labyrinth has captured the imagination of many visitors since opening in 1994. An underground boat takes you deep into the spectacular caverns beneath the Braichgoch mountain at Corris, near Machynlleth. As you walk through the caverns, Welsh tales of King Arthur are told with tableaux and stunning sound and light effects. The journey ends with a return trip along the beautiful subterranean river into the grounds of Corris Craft Centre.

The Craft Centre – the starting point for King Arthur's Labyrinth – is home to six craft workshops in which you can see first hand the skills employed in the creation of the many gift items on display. These include woodcraft, toys, jewellery, leather goods and handmade candles, and there is also a shop selling an attractive range of souvenirs, gifts and books on the Celtic Arthurian theme.

The Crwybr Restaurant offers full meals, teas and refreshments throughout the day, and there is also a picnic area and children's play area.

Visitors to King Arthur's Labyrinth are advised to wear warm clothing, as the underground caverns are cool. The 45-minute tour involves a walk of about half a mile along level gravel paths which are suitable for all but the very frail. However, the variety of craft shops, gardens and refreshments within the Corris Craft Centre – plus the stunning scenery of the valley – guarantees plenty of enjoyment for everyone.

Newtown

Newtown, in the centre of the Upper Severn Valley in Mid Wales, is the market town for a broad and fertile area. The wide central street leads down to the river and pleasant riverside promenade.

The old church stands near the bridge. The fine tower remains, but a new church was built in 1847 on the main road. The original church, however, has in its graveyard the tomb of Newtown's most famous son, Robert Owen. He was born here in 1771, and was a pioneer of enlightened capitalism in his New Lanark mills in Scotland, but gained his greatest fame as one of the fathers of the cooperative movement in Britain. He was also the founder of nursery schools. There is a Robert Owen Museum in Broad Street, and a small textile museum in one of the old hand-weaving factories in Commercial Street.

In the centre of the town several interesting architectural styles crowd the main shopping streets, including the ornate Barclays clock tower and a brick-and-timber W.H. Smith, restored to its early 20th-century elegance and housing a small exhibition about the famous firm on its upper floor. Older buildings can be seen in the side streets and squares leading towards the river.

Newtown has benefited by the establishment of new industries, including a Laura Ashley factory. It still, however retains an air of a busy market town. Next to the station is the large Royal Welsh Warehouse where, in 1859, Pryse Jones started the world's first mail-order scheme, selling Welsh flannel products. The beautiful 32-acre Dolerw Park lies over the river from the town, and is reached by a new footbridge across the Severn. Newtown also has its own little theatre which offers a varied programme of opera, drama and dance.

Behind the town, on the road to Llanfair Caereinion, is the church of Bettws Cedewain, with its 14th-century roof. From Bettws you can traverse the complicated and narrow roads to Gregynog Hall, four miles north of Newtown. It was the home of the Davies sisters, who made it a centre of the arts and music in the years after the First

World War. Here they established the Gregynog Press, producing editions much sought after by lovers of fine printing, and accumulated the remarkable collection of works by French impressionists which is in the National Museum at Cardiff. The Gregynog Press has been reinstated with assistance from the Welsh Arts Council.

About three miles north-east of Newtown, along twisting, narrow lanes off the A483 near Abermule, are the remains of Dolforwyn Castle, a Welsh fortress built by Llywelyn ap Gruffudd in 1273.

Davies Memorial Gallery For more information ring 01686 625041.

Newtown Textile Museum For further details contact the local Tourist Information Centre.

Robert Owen Memorial Museum For further details contact the local Tourist Information Centre.

W.H. Smith Museum This is located in High Street. For further information ring 01686 626280.

Dolforwyn Castle For further information contact the local Tourist Information Centre.

Theatr Hafren This excellent theatre offers a full and varied programme throughout the year – opera, dance, music, drama, comedy, children's shows, family entertainment and exhibitions of visual art. Facilities include the new Gallery Bar which is open outside performance hours and has twelve wheelchair spaces. In a convenient location near the town centre, and with parking for over 200 cars (including spaces for ANABL badge holders), Theatr Hafren is considered by many to be the best venue for arts and entertainment in Mid Wales and The Borders. To book, or for more information, ring the box office on 01686 625007.

Welshpool

A bustling market town with well-ordered streets which looks and feels more English than it does Welsh. There are half-timbered Tudor buildings and Georgian architecture to be found in this borderland town. It stands on the Montgomery Canal and visitors can enjoy trips along part of the canal's restored section.

Welshpool has two noteworthy churches. St Mary's stands on high ground overlooking the town, and dates back to the 13th century. The other church is located to the west of the town centre and commands views over the Severn Valley. The Powysland Museum has many interesting relics of the region, the most notable of which is an Iron Age shield.

Welshpool's crowning glory is Powis Castle, about 1 mile south-west of the town..

Powis Castle & Gardens For opening hours ring 01938 554336.

Powysland Museum & Montgomery Canal Centre For more information ring 01938 554656.

Welshpool & Llanfair Light Railway For more information ring 01938 810441.

If you like open space the Heart of Wales is the place to be. The soaring hills, remote forests and quiet valleys are a world away from the hectic pace of millennium life. Although not as well known by walkers as the neighbouring Brecon Beacons, the hills around areas such as Rhayader, Builth Wells and Llanwrtyd Wells are well worth exploring, and you don't have to get very far off the beaten track to get them all to yourself - even in the height of summer. This same area has also developed a reputation for the high quality of its mountain biking. A mix of open moorland trails, technical single track valleys and endless forest fire roads makes for some of the best off-road action in Wales.

The birdlife of the area also has a special attraction - there are many RSPB sites where rare species may be seen, and the success of the red kite in coming back from the brink of extinction here in its Welsh stronghold is obvious from the number of visitors who spot them hanging in the breeze.

Pony trekking and horse riding are also ideally suited to the Heart of Wales' open landscape, and this traditional means of transport is also one of the best for exploring the countryside. And for something a little more novel, how about bog snorkelling? The World Bog Snorkelling Championships, held every year in Llanwrtyd Wells, have put the town on the map, and from 1999 there'll also be a bog cycling championship (one to watch rather than do, perhaps!).

Below is a quick guide to where you can find all types of outdoor action in the area, from walking to golfing, swimming to - yes, you guessed it, bog snorkelling!

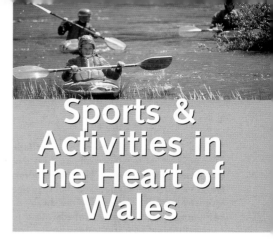

Sports & Activities in the Heart of Wales

Climbing

MB Outdoor Pursuit Services, Llandrindod Wells For further information ring 01597 825671.

Golf

Builth Wells Golf Club A superb 18-hole course and a unique clubhouse are the big attractions for golfers at Builth Wells. The clubhouse occupies a converted 16th-century Welsh longhouse (still boasting several original features) which during its fascinating history has also served as a mansion, a pub and a farm. For more information ring the clubhouse on 01982 553296 or the club professional on 553293.

Knighton Golf Course Tel: 01597 528656.

Llandrindod Wells Golf Club A superbly designed 18-hole course offering spectacular views, excellent hospitality and a variety of challenging holes – all at realistic prices. The clubhouse overlooks the lake, and facilities include bar, restaurant, changing rooms, showers and well-stocked gift shop. For more information ring 01597 823873.

Maesmawr Golf Club Mid Wales Golf Centre, Caersws. For further information ring 01686 688303.

Bowling

Radnor Indoor Bowling Centre, Llandrindod Wells For more information ring 01597 825014.

Bro Ddyfi Leisure Centre, Machynlleth
This superb Centre is open all day every day
and caters for all ages. The outstanding
facilities include mother and baby room,
extensive catering, access for the disabled,
swimming pool, sauna, sunbeds, fitness
suite, climbing wall and indoor bowls. For
more information ring 01654 703300.

Builth Wells Indoor Swimming Pool
For more information ring 01982 552603.

Builth Wells Sports Centre The Centre
is open all through school holidays and at
weekends, and in the evenings during term
time. Facilities include multi-purpose sports
hall, squash courts and fitness and health
suites. For more information ring 01982
552324.

**Caereinion Leisure Centre, Llanfair
Caereinion, near Welshpool**. The Centre
caters for a wide range of recreational
activities, from badminton to squash. For
more information ring 01938 810634.

**East Radnor Leisure Centre,
Presteigne** Family activity and fun all year
round is on offer here. The swimming pool is
heated to 86°F (30°C) and there are daily
Monster Fun Sessions. Other attractions for
youngsters include multi-sport activity
sessions, roller discos, soft play adventure
and a bouncy castle, and you can also enjoy
the sauna, squash courts, fitness studio and
sports hall. For more information ring 01544
260302.

Flash Leisure Centre, Welshpool The
most extensive leisure facility in Mid Wales,
with leisure pool and flume, rapids ride,
jacuzzi, beach area, swim lanes, covered

restaurant, health suite (sauna, steam room
and sunbeds), fitness suite (full range of
cardio-vascular and resistance equipment),
indoor bowls and a great deal more. For
further information ring 01938 555952.

Knighton Leisure Centre This
developing Centre has a 20-metre swimming
pool, fitness suite, squash courts, tennis
courts, fast-tanning sunbed and soft play
area. Others activities include 5-a-side
soccer, basketball and netball. For more
information ring 01547 529187.

Llandrindod Wells Sports Centre
Adjacent to the town's high school campus,
overlooking the River Ithon, the Centre
boasts a 20-metre swimming pool, large
multi-purpose sports hall, floodlit playing
area and grass pitches. Activities include
aerobics and splash dance, and the Centre
also manages the lakeside putting green,
crazy golf and lake fishery. For more
information ring 01597 824249.

Llanfyllin Sports Centre The Centre
caters for all ages, with regular courses and
activities year round to suit all abilities. For
more information ring 01691 648814.

Llanidloes Sports Centre The Centre
provides the ideal opportunity for the whole
family to indulge in leisure activities old and
new. The best in sport and recreational
facilities and a warm welcome make the
Centre a very popular attraction. For more
information ring 01686 412871.

Maldwyn Leisure Centre, Newtown
Catering for all ages and abilities, the Centre
hosts both local and international events and
boasts a new fully-floodlit hockey pitch and
athletics track. The extensive facilities also
include swimming pool and lounge bar. For
more information ring 01686 628771.

Rhayader Leisure Centre The ideal venue for leisure, parties, receptions and meetings, with all facilities, including swimming pool, available for club or group hire. From children's birthday parties to full-scale discos, the Centre can cater for every occasion. For more information ring 01597 811013.

Mountain Biking

Clive Powell Mountain Bikes The unspoilt area around the Elan Valley, with its dramatic dams and miles of glorious open countryside, is the perfect retreat for mountain biking. Many of the byways and bridleways, once used for hauling peat and herding sheep and taking goods to market, now provide the challenge of lung-bursting climbs and exhilarating descents. Clive Powell Mountain Bikes offer a friendly service, with guides who will help you select routes to match your ability and experience. Advice and tuition are also available. For more information ring 01597 810585 or 811343.

Red Kite Mountain Bike Centre Based at the Neuadd Arms Hotel in Llanwrtyd Wells, the Centre is the ideal place from which to explore the southern end of the Cambrian Mountains - 'the Lake District of Wales'. There is a wide choice of routes to suit all abilities , ages and ambitions, with bike hire available by the day or half day. The hotel can also offer you accommodation - from bed and breakfast to full board - for a complete biking break or holiday at any time of year. You are also welcome to bring your own bike. For more information ring 01591 610236.

Sporting Breaks

Mid Wales Leisure Breaks This joint venture was formed recently by three established tourist attractions in the scenic Severn Valley. On offer are mini leisure breaks to suit all age groups, and the package includes two nights' accommodation and participation in three sports. If your accommodation is hotel-based, dinner is also included.

The sports comprise quad trekking (including instruction, safety briefing, helmets and waterproofs); golf (on a superb 9-hole course, with a practice range to try your skills beforehand); and clay pigeon shooting (where you will receive a brief introduction to the sport, personal instruction, and 50 clays and cartridges).

Each of the three attractions operating Mid Wales Leisure Breaks is a family-run business, and all visitors are guaranteed a warm and friendly welcome. For more information ring 01686 688303.

Walking

Welsh Wayfaring Holidays Based at the Neuadd Arms Hotel, Llanwrtyd Wells, these holidays will appeal to visitors who enjoy a pleasant day's guided walk through some of the most outstanding countryside Wales has to offer - comforted by the knowledge that awaiting them at the end of their exertions are all the pleasures of a relaxing, well-run hotel, including excellent food. There is a good choice of walks to suit all abilities and experience. For more information ring 01591 610236.

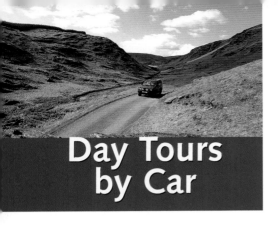

Day Tours by Car

Tour 1

Brecon-Builth Wells-Llangammarch Wells-Llanwrtyd Wells-Llandovery-Brecon 64 miles

From Brecon take the A438, signposted Hereford. At the Bulls Head Hotel turn left, then on to the B4520 Upper Chapel road and pass the cathedral. Follow the road to Lower Chapel. After Upper Chapel, on the southern edge of the Mynydd Eppynt hills, turn right on to the B4520. At the summit (1,370 ft) there are outstanding views over the hills. In Builth Wells turn left, joining the A483 Llandovery road, and cross the River Irfon. Continue along the valley to the village of Garth, turning left on to the unclassified Llangammarch Wells road. Just outside Llangammarch Wells turn right for Llanwrtyd Wells, crossing the river. After about a mile turn left, following the railway into Llanwrtyd Wells, and turn left to rejoin the A483.

Nr Llandovery

There is a gradual climb up to the edge of Crychan Forest and to the Sugar Loaf (1,000 ft), which stands at the head of the Bran Valley. Descend towards Llandovery, where there is an unclassified road on your right, signposted Rhandirmwyn. This 12-mile stretch along the Tywi Valley enjoys spectacular hill scenery as you approach the Llyn Brianne Reservoir and Dam. From the viewing point a narrow road leads high above the shores for 7 miles into the Tywi Forest. Situated between the rivers Tywi and Bran, is the pleasant market town of Llandovery, with its ruined Norman castle. From the town take the A40 towards Brecon, which takes you through the deep, wooded valley of the Afon Gwydderig.

Beyond Trecastle you will follow the River Usk for the short distance to Sennybridge. After the village turn right onto the A4057, and at Defynnog bear left onto the A4215 Merthyr road. Continue along the Senni Valley, which will give you fine views ahead of Fan Frynych (2,047 ft) and other Fforest Fawr hills. After 2¾ miles turn left at the signpost for the Mountain Centre on to a narrow road crossing the Mynydd Illtud (1,100 ft). To the right there are sweeping views of the Brecon Beacons, with the main summits of Pen-y-Fan (2,906 ft) and Corn Du (2,863 ft) clearly visible. The Mountain Centre is a Brecon Beacons National Park information centre, with a viewing gallery and picnic area. From the centre the road gradually descends, offering fine views of the Black Mountains, and on reaching the A40 turn right for Brecon.

Tour 2

Brecon-Merthyr Tydfil-Talybont-Crickhowell-Brecon 63 miles

Leave Brecon on the A40 (Llandovery road), crossing the River Usk. After about a mile take the second exit at the roundabout and then take the the next left turn, signposted Mountain Centre. The road climbs up to moorland, with excellent views of the Brecon Beacons, the summits of Pen-y-Fan (2,906 ft) and Corn Du (2,863 ft) clearly visible.

Pass the entrance to the Mountain Centre (a national park information centre and picnic site) and after a mile, at the crossroads, turn left on to the A4215, with Fan Frynych (2,047 ft) rising straight ahead. After 3 miles the road descends into the Tarell Valley; turn right on to the A470, signposted Merthyr. There is then an easy ascent to a summit of 1,440 ft, with Fan Fawr (2,409 ft) ahead. On the left after 1/2 mile is the starting point of footpaths to the main peaks, and the road descends along the wooded Taff Valley, passing three reservoirs before reaching the edge of Merthyr. Continue to Cefn-coed-y-cymmer on the outskirts of Merthyr Tydfil and then turn left on to the Pontsticill and Talybont road. After passing under a railway bridge turn left. (Turning right will take you on a short detour to the ruins of 13th-century Morlais Castle.) Continues through Pontsticill, and at the end of the village keep left to follow the shores of the Taf Fechan Reservoir. Ahead there are distant views of the lower Brecon Beacon summits. After 2¾ miles the route turns right, but for the Neuadd Reservoirs (below the Beacons) go straight on. On the ascent to a 1,400 ft summit, the site of the former Torpantau Station – 1,350 ft above sea level – is passed on the left. At the top there are views to the left of Craig y Fan-ddu (2,224 ft) and Craig y Fan (2,502 ft) before a long steep descent through woodland to the Talybont Valley. With 2,000-ft hills on the left and the prominent 1,806-ft peak of Tor-y-Foel ahead, the drive follows the two-miles-long Talybont Reservoir. About 1¼ mile beyond the reservoir, turn right – no signpost – into Talybont village.

The road then crosses the restored

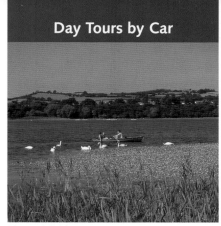

Llangorse Lake

Brecon and Abergavenny Canal. Turn right on to the B4558 – no signpost – and beyond the village follow the signposts for Llangynidr and Crickhowell, along the lovely wooded Usk Valley. Beyond the canal bridge at the edge of Llangynidr, turn right on to the B4560 Beaufort road. The road climbs through sharp bends to 1,460 ft , with magnificent views across the Usk Valley to the Black Mountain. Also to be seen are Mynydd Llangorse (1,700 ft), Pen Cerrig-Calch (2,302 ft), Pen Allt-Mawr (2,360 ft), Crug Mawr (1,805 ft) and the famous Sugar Loaf (1,955 ft). Passing a quarry, turn left on to an unclassified road signposted Crickhowell and descend to recross the canal at Llangattock. At the end of the village turn left on to the A4077, then right to cross the Usk by an attractive bridge into Crickhowell - a town with several Georgian houses and a restored 14th-century church. Leave on the A40 Brecon road. After 2¾ miles the road passes a right turn to the hamlet of Tretower, with its picturesque manor house and ruined castle. After 2½ miles the road climbs to Bwlch and good views of the Usk Valley. Beyond the village, at the war memorial, turn right on to the B4560 Talgarth road, passing along high ground below Mynydd Llangorse (1,700 ft). To the left is Llangorse Lake - the second largest natural lake in Wales. At the end of Llangorse village turn left on to the little country road (which takes you towards Brecon), shortly after passing a road to the lakeside. After 1½ miles turn left across a bridge and pass through Llanfihangel Tal-y-Llyn. After 2½ miles, turn left. After ½ mile turn right on to the A40 to return to Brecon alongside the Brecon and Abergavenny Canal.

Tour 3

Abergavenny-Llanthony-Hay-on-Wye-Bronllys-Talgarth-Crickhowell-Abergavenny 40 miles

Leave Abergavenny on the main A465, signposted Hereford. In the village of Llanfihangel turn left on to the B4423, up the beautiful valley of the Afon Honddu. Sights worth viewing en route up the valley include a detour to the hamlet of Cwmyoy (boasting "the crookedest church in Wales"); Llanthony, with its beautiful priory; and Capel-y-ffin, with its picturesque little white church. The road climbs over the Black Mountains through the narrow Gospel Pass – the second highest road in Wales. There are extensive views on the long descent from the summit. After about 5 miles, at a T-junction, turn right onto the B4350 road into Hay-on-Wye.

From Hay-on-Wye, turn left to join the B4351, signposted Hereford, to the village of Clyro. Here turn left on to the A438, signposted Brecon, through the pretty villages of Llowes and Glasbury. At the T-junction, turn right for Three Cocks and Bronllys. Turn left onto the A479, signposted Abergavenny, passing the ruins of Bronllys Castle.

At Talgarth, turn right across the bridge and then left. The road then climbs through the Black Mountains and eventually descends into the village of Tretower, where you turn left on to the A40 for Crickhowell and, through beautiful scenery, to Abergavenny.

Tour 4

Rhayader-Elan Valley-Devil's Bridge-Llangurig-Rhayader 60 miles

Leave Rhayader on the B4518 for the highly attractive Elan Valley reservoirs, built from 1892 onwards for Birmingham Corporation. At the edge of Elan village the road climbs to the Caban Coch Dam and Reservoir and on to the Garreg-Ddu viaduct; turn left to cross it on the road to the Claerwen Reservoir, opened in 1952. Pass through pleasant woodland and along the attractive Claerwen Valley, turning right to reach the Claerwen Dam. Return along the same road to the Garreg-Ddu viaduct and turn left, following the wooded shores of Garreg-Ddu Reservoir. At the end is a short, winding climb which leads to the Penygarreg Dam and Reservoir. Beyond is the dam of Craig Goch Reservoir. The water stretches out beside the road as the drive passes through pleasant moorland before climbing to turn left on to the Aberystwyth road .

The road follows the River Elan to reach the 1,320-ft summit before the long descent into the Ystwyth valley. After 3¾ miles you pass the site of former lead and silver mines. Beyond Cwmystwyth the road climbs again to join the B4574 Devil's Bridge road, giving views of the Rheidol Valley ahead and the deep Mynach Valley on the right. The descent continues to Devil's Bridge, with its spectacular waterfalls and three bridges built in a stack. Turn sharp right on to the A4120 Ponterwyd road, crossing Devil's Bridge. After 2¾ miles turn right on to the B4343 Dyffryn Castell road, which climbs to 1,000 ft above the main A44 road. Take the A44 towards Llangurig to climb out of the Castell Valley. Eisteddfa Gurig, at the 1,400 ft summit, is the starting point of several beautiful walks and pony trails to the 2,470 ft summit of Plynlimon - the source of the

River Wye. The River Severn rises three miles further north. On the long descent the road follows the River Tarenig before the River Wye joins it from the left, with good views as you approach Llangurig, a pretty village attractively situated at over 900 ft. Bear right, with Rhayader signposted on to the A470, and enjoy the pleasant drive down the Wye Valley back to Rhayader.

Tour 5

Llanidloes-Machynlleth-Llanidloes56 miles

Leave Llanidloes on the B4518 Llyn Clywedog road and cross the River Severn, turning left to follow the Clywedog Valley. After about 2 miles, with the 1,580 ft Fan Hill on your right, turn left. Cross the valley and ascend to the Clywedog Dam - at 237 ft. the highest in Britain, opened in 1968. There is a viewing area on the right. There are further views of the reservoir before the road enters the extensive Hafren Forest. At the T-junction turn right on to the Llanbrynmair road. After 23⁄4 miles, near Staylittle, turn left on to the B4518, and 3⁄4 of a mile later turn left on to the unclassified Machynlleth road. After a short distance you pass high above the deep, V-shaped gorge of the River Twymyn on the right. Continue to the former mine workings at the remote hamlet of Dylife. A long climb to moorland 1,700 ft high gives wide, distant mountain views.

On the descent the views are even more impressive. Beyond a range of 2,000 ft hills above the Dovey Valley are the distant summits of Cader Idris (2,927 ft), 14 miles away, and Aran Mawddwy (2,970 ft), 16 miles away - the highest Welsh summit outside Snowdonia. After a long, easy descent, keep straight on at all road junctions before dropping more steeply into the wooded Dulas Valley. Proceed to the pleasant market town of Machynlleth, which

lies in the Dovey Valley and is dominated by its massive clock tower. Leave the town on the A489 Newtown road, passing through Penegoes before re-entering the Dovey Valley to the Cemmaes Road. There are superb views up the valley towards Mallwyd before the road turns away on the A470 Newtown road to continue up the Twymyn Valley. At Llanbrynmair the river turns south and tributaries join from the north and east, one of which - the River Laen - is followed by this route as the road climbs through a wooded gorge to the summit at Talerddig, 700 ft above Machynlleth. Follow the broad Carno Valley through Carno and go on through Clatter and Pont-dolgoch to reach Caersws on the River Severn. Continue on the A470, and after 3⁄4 of a mile turn right at the T-junction on to the Llangurig road. Pass over a level crossing and follow the River Severn through Llandinam, the birthplace of David Davies, who did much to develop railways and coal-mining in Wales. His statue can be seen to the right on the way back to Llanidloes.

Llandrindod Wells

Index

ACKNOWLEDGEMENTS

The author's thanks are due to John Norris, Brecon Beacons National Park, Glyn Davies, Clare Price (Lily Publications), Neil Price & Andrew Lowe and the staff of Haven Colourprint; and David Lemon and all the advertisers.